Louisburg Library
Bringing People and Information Together

3D PRINTING

THE REVOLUTION IN
PERSONALIZED MANUFACTURING

MELISSA KOCH

TWENTY-FIRST CENTURY BOOKS / MINNEAPOLIS

To my grandfather, Lewis N. Higbee, and to all
innovative spirits who love making things

Acknowledgments: Thank you to Maxim Lobovsky, Nadia Cheng, Hasti Afsarifard, Carlos Olguin, Amos Dudley, the HP 3D printing team, and Autodesk 3D printing, specifically Guillermo Melantoni and Sarah O'Rourke, for sharing and showing me their 3D printing expertise.

Thank you to Natalie and Judi Kledzik, Mona Sabet, and members of my children's book critique group for all your reviews. A special thank-you to Susan Casey, Lisa Pampuch, and Marianne Wallace for encouraging me throughout the writing process.

Thank you to San Mateo Public Libraries for their resources and helpful staff, the UnaMesa Association for providing a serene place to write, and our babysitter, Kristi Fredrick, for being there whenever we needed her.

A special thank-you to my husband and son for giving me space and time to write and lots of ideas on how to tell the 3D printing story.

Twenty-First Century Books
A division of Lerner Publishing Group, Inc.
241 First Avenue North
Minneapolis, MN 55401 USA

For reading levels and more information, look up this title at www.lernerbooks.com.

Main body text set in Adobe Garamond Pro 11/15.
Typeface provided by Adobe Systems.

Library of Congress Cataloging-in-Publication Data

Names: Koch, Melissa, author.
Title: 3D Printing : the revolution in personalized manufacturing / by Melissa Koch.
Description: Minneapolis : Twenty-First Century Books, [2017] | Includes bibliographical references and
    index.
Identifiers: LCCN 2016033030 (print) | LCCN 2016033530 (ebook) | ISBN 9781512415704
    (lb : alk. paper) | ISBN 9781512448603 (eb pdf)
Subjects: LCSH: Three-dimensional printing—Juvenile literature.
Classification: LCC TS171.95 .K63 2017 (print) | LCC TS171.95 (ebook) | DDC 621.9/88—dc23

LC record available at https://lccn.loc.gov/2016033030

Manufactured in the United States of America
1-39927-21393-3/21/2017

CONTENTS

WASPS DO IT

The rhythmic buzzing and continuous oozing of a 3D (three-dimensional) printer can draw a crowd. Hypnotized, everyone watches as the printer deposits small bits of material, layer upon layer on a platform until slowly a new object emerges. Ready to use.

3D printing may sound like science fiction. There's a reason for that: 3D printing has been a star of science fiction in television and film. For example, the technology appeared in scenes in *Star Trek*, the popular 1960s TV series. Later, in the 1980s' TV show *Star Trek: The Next Generation*, the 3D printer was named the Replicator. In this series, crew members on the Starship *Enterprise* could order up and print anything they wanted. Viewers wished they had their own Replicators to make pizza and banana splits. In the twenty-first century, MakerBot even named its popular 3D printer Replicator.

We humans began actually experimenting with 3D printing in the 1980s. This style of printing is also known as additive manufacturing because it adds materials layer upon layer to create a 3D object. But humans were not the first to develop 3D printing. Wasps were additive manufacturers long before us. The method paper wasps use to build their homes reveals the basics of 3D printing.

HUMAN WASP ENGINEERS

Wasps live in nests in communities called colonies. A queen wasp starts a colony by building a nest. She uses her mandibles (appendages near the mouth) to scrape wood pulp from trees, fence posts, and even cardboard into her mouth. Mixed with her saliva, these materials become a watery pulp. The queen finds a good location for building the nest. She spits out the pulp, layer by layer, to create hexagonal (six-sided) cells in which her young will develop. As the number of wasps in the colony grows, the new generations of worker wasps construct new cells the same way the queen did.

In 2012 an engineering team in Italy known as the World's Advanced Saving Project (WASP) closely watched wasps, specifically the mud dauber wasp, at work. The human WASP team decided to build 3D printers to mimic the wasps' technique. The WASP engineers collect large chunks of clay, sand, plant, and other soil materials and put them into a custom-made, 20-foot-tall (6-meter) 3D printer to print a house, layer by layer. The house

Wasps build the hexagonal cells of their colonies in layers. Inspired by this natural technology, human entrepreneurs have modeled 3D printing techniques to build houses and other structures layer by layer.

cost almost nothing to print because the nontraditional building materials are gathered at the site. The team creates these homes at locations where typical building materials (bricks, stones, and wood) are inaccessible or too costly to use for homes and other buildings.

3D printing can change not only where people live but how they live. For example, high school students in Van Buren, Ohio, used a 3D printer to create a prosthetic hand for a toddler in their town. The students gathered thirty dollars' worth of plastic, melted it into liquid form, and put it into the school's 3D printer. They used 3D computer-aided design (CAD) software to design the hand. Thomas Wolford, a senior at Van Buren High School, described the printing process. "The nozzle goes around it all in crazy funky patterns and prints it out layer by layer," he said. Another senior, Aaron Scasny, added, "We ran fishing wire down through the bottom [of the hand] and this elastic threaded cord through the top, so when you bend it, it acts like tendons in your hand." Because young children outgrow their prosthetics, outfitting them with artificial limbs was expensive in the past. But 3D printing has made it possible for more children and adults to have the prosthetics they need because they can afford it.

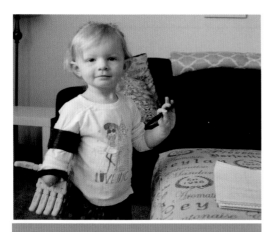

Teens in Ohio 3D printed a prosthetic hand for Addy Johnson at their school. The technologies involved in 3D printing are available to all and are often used to improve everyday life for individuals.

BIOPRINTERS

In the medical field, 3D printing is a modern superpower. With bioprinters, bioprinting researchers from all over the world have successfully re-created human ears, noses, skull bones, tracheas, bladders, and other body parts. The ink-jet printing of viable cells is one example of what a 3D printer can do. It deposits drops of

This 3D printer can quickly produce human tissues. The bioprint head moves back and forth, and up and down, placing human cells on the platform. The bioprinter alternates layers of bioink (a dissolvable gel) with the cells to protect them during printing. It also places growth factor (a protein or a hormone) in the solution to help cells grow. The final tissue takes several hours to print.

human cellular material and proteins onto a platform in the same way an ink-jet printer drops ink onto a piece of paper. Traditional printers place one layer of ink onto one sheet of paper at a time. By contrast, a 3D ink-jet printer adjusts its platform up and down adding cellular material, layer by layer, until a 3D organ emerges.

In the future, 3D medical printouts could be lifesaving for people who need organ transplants or repairs due to injuries or illness. However, Robert Langer, a professor of chemical engineering at Massachusetts Institute of Technology (MIT), cautions about the current limitations of 3D bioprinting. "Right now, we can't make any organ or tissue to function properly in humans other than skin. 3D printing hasn't even been used successfully for that. Making an organ also requires blood vessels, nerves, and cells to behave properly. 3D printing can't do that." Bioprinting researchers worldwide continue their laboratory work: researching, designing, and 3D printing to find lifesaving solutions.

Wasps have had millions of years to evolve their 3D printing process. For humans 3D printing technologies are a revolution.

CHAPTER 1
INVENTING 3D PRINTING

Innovative ideas often occur to more than one person at the same time. And it usually takes more than one person's efforts to make an innovative idea a reality. 3D printing got its start with Chuck Hull, Scott Crump, and Carl Deckard. These engineers did not know one another when they each invented 3D printing, but they had a lot in common. They each worked in manufacturing. They each saw that traditional manufacturing needed a new and faster approach to developing prototypes. Prototypes are demonstration objects that resemble the final product to help developers refine a product before they build it.

Engineers and designers use prototyping to create a mockup of a part to see how well it will work. CAD software helps engineers and designers make prototypes so they can test their designs. At some point in the process, designers must make and test the actual physical prototype. Often building and testing a design happens many times before the designed product actually works. Using traditional manufacturing approaches of building, welding, and assembling a prototype is costly and time consuming. Hull, Crump, and Deckard saw the need to speed up prototyping. They knew that rapid prototyping would reduce

the time and cost of developing a new product. These quickly made prototypes would have enough of the features of the final product to help designers and engineers make changes to the design so they could build the best product possible. Independently of one another, the three men successfully developed 3D printing processes that are still in use.

MEET CHUCK HULL

In 1983 Charles (Chuck) Hull had been experimenting for months with a technique called stereolithography (SLA). This printing method requires a computer, an ultraviolet (UV) laser, and a liquid goo called photopolymer resin. The resin naturally hardens when it comes in contact with the heat of the laser's light. Hull was working for a company in San Gabriel, California, developing durable resin coatings for tabletops. His experiments with the resin gave him the idea that he could turn his digital designs into physical objects using those same resins. His company agreed to give him a small lab to see what he could make. Hull imagined that he could create a process for engineers to quickly make prototypes for the objects they wanted to

To be successful, an invention has to be more than a good idea. It has to be designed well and work well. So before making a product, a company will first develop a prototype (*above*), or model, to make sure the idea will work as planned, look good, and be cost-effective to manufacture. This can be a lengthy, expensive process, however. 3D printing can speed it up significantly and save companies money too.

These decorative pieces are 3D printed through stereolithography. This method uses photopolymer resins, which harden when exposed to ultraviolet light.

manufacture. After many disappointing attempts, suddenly, late one night, he turned the goo into a cup. He used software on his computer to draw the cup, and he used the laser to harden the resin and to print the cup layer by layer. Excitedly, he called his wife, Antoinette, and asked her to drive to the lab to see what he had created. She, in her pajamas and ready for bed, said, "This had better be good!"

Years later, when interviewed about that moment, Antoinette said, "He held this part in his hand and he said 'I did it. The world as we know [it] will never be the same.' We laughed and we cried and we stayed up all night just imagining."

Hull started his own 3D printing company, 3D Systems, in 1986. He went on to receive the first patent for 3D printing using stereolithography, the technology behind his cup. He also received several other patents for 3D technologies and developed STL, the stereolithography file format that many 3D printers use.

SLA, STL, AND CAD

3D PRINTING RELIES ON THESE BASIC TECHNOLOGIES:

- **STEREOLITHOGRAPHY (SLA).** This was the first 3D printing process and continues to be widely used. SLA remains popular because the technique produces a smooth object. Other 3D techniques can show individual layers of material, often resulting in a bumpy, unfinished look.

  In an SLA printer, a UV laser is focused on a tub of UV-curable photopolymer resin to produce a layer on the build platform. Then the printer lowers the build platform slightly for the next layer, and the process is repeated until the object is fully formed. This high-quality process comes at a high price for the printer and the resin material. Originally, organizations used SLA for commercial purposes only. Since then companies such as Formlabs, 3D Systems, and others have provided desktop SLA printers at more affordable prices for individual professionals.

- **STEREOLITHOGRAPHY FILE FORMAT (STL).** Chuck Hull developed the STL file format for his SLA files. A file format stores specific types of information. For example, a JPEG file format contains data for displaying an image. A pdf contains data for sharing a document across platforms. For 3D printing, Hull wanted to invent a file format that would allow a 3D printer to read a CAD file. He called it STL, another abbreviation for stereolithography. STL has become the standard 3D printing file format.

- **COMPUTER-AIDED DESIGN (CAD).** Engineers and designers in many fields use CAD software to create two- or three-dimensional (2D or 3D) digital representations of physical objects on their computers. They can use those designs to determine how best to build the object. With 3D printing, they can design the object using CAD, save the information as an STL file, and then print the object from a 3D printer.

MEET SCOTT CRUMP

In the late 1980s, Scott Crump knew that engineers at his company needed a way to develop prototypes easily and rapidly to test new product designs. He had been thinking about how he could give engineers a way to create a physical object from a CAD file. At home in Eden Prairie, Minnesota, Crump had been experimenting with creating a toy frog for his two-year-old daughter. One day, he was successful. He made a frog with a hot glue gun and a CAD program.

Scott Crump, pictured here with a 3D-printed motorbike, cofounded Stratasys with his wife, Lisa, in suburban Minneapolis, Minnesota. He came up with the idea for fused deposition modeling, in which a printer head places (or deposits) layers of melted plastic on a movable platform.

Crump realized he could automate the process through fused deposition modeling (FDM). In FDM a 3D printer heats a thermoplastic—a plastic that becomes pliable when heated and hard when cooled—to a semiliquid state. The printer then places the plastic in layers of small beads on a platform along a predetermined path. If the printed object has fragile pieces, the 3D printer produces a removable support during the printing process. When the project is fully printed, the support is then removed and the 3D object is ready to use.

Crump refined FDM in his kitchen, ruining most of his family's pans to melt the plastics. When their food started tasting like plastic, his wife, Lisa, asked him to move his work to the garage. Seeing her husband's passion and the possibilities for FDM, she encouraged him to turn his expensive hobby into a business.

In 1998 Scott and Lisa Crump started the 3D printing company Stratasys. They filed several 3D patents, including patents for FDM, and developed many 3D printers. FDM is also known as fused filament fabrication (FFF) when the process is used by non-Stratasys companies. It is one of the most popular 3D printing processes for individual users. Two decades later, Stratasys, like 3D Systems, sells a range of 3D printers and 3D printing services to many industries. So far, the Crumps' company has more than twenty-four different 3D printers. Collectively, those 3D printers use more than 120 different materials. Stratasys enables companies and individuals to 3D print prototypes, concept models, molds, and actual parts. These 3D printers cost from $2,000 to more than $600,000. Stratasys has more than 560 patents pending or granted.

MEET CARL DECKARD

In the summer of 1981, Carl Deckard had just finished his first year of college at the University of Texas at Austin. He had started a summer job at TRW Mission, a manufacturing shop that made parts for drilling oil. Deckard was intrigued that TRW was using CAD, then a new software tool. He saw an opportunity to create 3D parts for manufacturing using a computer. He thought about it for more than two years until he had an idea he thought would work.

In 1984, in his senior year of college, Deckard approached Joe Beaman, a mechanical engineering professor, with an idea. Deckard realized he could use a directed energy beam (such as a laser) to melt together particles of powder, such as metals or plastics. Deckard thought it would be possible to make a part from the melted powdered material. An added plus: he wanted to go to graduate school, and he needed a graduate school project. Beaman liked the idea and agreed to work with Deckard to develop selective laser sintering (SLS). Together, they wrote grants to fund their research and development work on SLS at the University of Texas.

To prove that SLS would work, Deckard did most of the work by hand. He used a device similar to a saltshaker to fill a small box with powder. A computer on the same table as the shaker ran the scanner whose laser beams would heat the powder. What did Deckard make? Chunks of plastic. From there, Deckard and Beaman developed a 3D printer that they called Betsy. Then they developed Godzilla, a machine that was too large and whose design tried to do too much. The two inventors abandoned Godzilla. Instead, they simplified their design and built Bambi, a reference to the short animated science-fiction cartoon film "Bambi Meets Godzilla" (1969). Students and professors at the University of Texas used Bambi for many years for research and project work.

Meanwhile, Deckard and Beaman wanted to go beyond their university work and start a business to sell their SLS machines. In 1986 the two men and investors started what became DTM, an SLS 3D printing company. In 2001, 3D Systems bought DTM. SLA and SLS technologies are similar. However, SLS is the only 3D printing process that can make metal objects as strong as traditionally manufactured metal objects. SLS is also the most complicated and costly of the three 3D printing processes.

For the material to build objects, SLS uses powdered material in a vat rather than liquids. High-powered lasers melt powdered particles together into a solid mass. SLS can work with any material that can be powdered and melted with a laser. This includes metals, ceramics, and plastics. An SLS printer then deposits pieces of the melted material, layer by layer, onto a platform in the vat until the product is complete. The SLS method doesn't require support structures since the powder in the vat

WHAT IS A PATENT?

A patent is a document that protects owners of an invention from having their inventions used without their permission. Governments issue patents so that anyone who wants to make, use, or sell a patented device, process, or application has to either pay the owner of the patent or get the owner's written permission.

In the United States, getting a patent takes time and money, so not everyone finishes the process. Those who do benefit professionally and financially from having a patent. For example, Chuck Hull was not the only person who filed a patent on a 3D printing process. An engineer in France and another in Japan also filed similar SLA patents. But they did not follow through. The US Patent Office granted Hull his patent for SLA in 1986, which helped him to start and grow his company, 3D Systems. Hull holds the first 3D printing patent: US Patent 4,575,330, Apparatus for Production of Three-Dimensional Objects by Stereolithography.

Hull did not patent the STL file format, however. So anyone who wants to adopt STL as their file format for 3D printing can do so legally without seeking permission first. STL has become the standard file format for all 3D printers and other forms of digital manufacturing as well.

Both Crump and Deckard filed patents on their 3D printing processes, which helped them to develop 3D printing companies. Crump filed the patent for FDM—US Patent 5,121,329, Apparatus and Method for Creating Three-Dimensional Objects. Deckard filed US Patent 5,155,324, Method for Selective Laser Sintering with Layerwise Cross-Scanning.

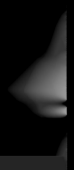

supports the object as it is being printed. The final product has a porous texture similar to a sponge.

TOGETHER, THEY STARTED A REVOLUTION

Hull, Crump, and Deckard started 3D printing as a way to help engineers with rapid prototyping and to more quickly manufacture parts. By the twenty-first century, their innovations touch more lives and more professionals in more fields than they imagined.

> **"I KNOW THIS: WHEN YOU GET ENOUGH SMART PEOPLE WORKING ON SOMETHING, IT ALWAYS GETS BETTER."**
>
> —Chuck Hull, founder of 3D Systems

Professionals in many industries—health care, architecture, automotive, aerospace, energy, clothing, dentistry, and culinary—use 3D print prototypes, concept models, molds, and actual parts.

In health care, doctors can print a replacement jawbone for a patient who has been injured in an accident. Architects can create a concept model of a building to better understand how the structural elements will work together. They can use what they learn from concept models to improve their designs and build buildings that are functional, safe, and beautiful. Automotive manufacturers can use a 3D printer to create molds—containers into which hot liquids are poured to take a specific shape and to harden as the liquids cool. They can use the molds multiple times to create automotive parts.

In aerospace, engineers can 3D print a fuel tank that will hold enough fuel for a satellite to stay in orbit for twenty or more years. Technologists 3D print new energy-efficient tools to power and purify water in remote locations. Shoemakers can help consumers to customize their shoes for the perfect design and fit. Orthodontists can print customized invisible aligners for their patients. Then, in some cases, a person can avoid wearing highly visible metal braces. Chefs at culinary institutes can use a 3D printer and chocolate to create hundreds of 3D chocolate trees that would be difficult or impossible to do by hand. These 3D printers redefine what it means to play with your food!

SLA, FDM, and SLS launched the 3D printing revolution and continue to be popular 3D printing processes. Hull, Crump, and Deckard are friends as well as competitors. When asked about all the innovations in 3D printing, Hull says, "I'm not a futurist. I don't have a crystal ball that tells me what things are going to happen, but I know this: when you get enough smart people working on something, it always gets better."

CHAPTER 2

HOW IT WORKS

The technology of 3D printing is a bit like cooking. You have a technique or process (Italian or Chinese cooking) that influences the specific materials (pizza dough or rice) used and dictates the hardware (pizza oven or wok). It has software (a recipe) and a file format (cooking instructions, such as the oven temperature and time), all of which you use to make something to eat. In 3D printing, the technique or process dictates the materials, hardware, software, and file format you will use to make the object you want. And just as with cooking, the hardware is a lot bigger if you cook for hundreds of people rather than for just you and your family. Some 3D printers would barely fit in your living room, while others are small enough to fit in your backpack.

THE BASICS

The ingredients of any 3D-printed object include a process, materials, hardware, software, and file format. How do these ingredients interact in 3D printing? With the software, you create a digital image of the object you want to create (the recipe). You then save the digital image in a 3D printing file format (the cooking instructions). The file format does two things: it slices your digital object into thin horizontal slices, or layers, like a deli worker slices cheese from a large cheese block. The file format then provides instructions to the hardware—the 3D printer—for how to add each layer on top of the previous layer so the printer can build the physical object you designed on your computer. Depending on the 3D printing process, the printer will squeeze melted material out of a nozzle (like a baker squeezing icing out of a cake-decorating tube). Or a laser will harden and deposit material layer by layer (like chocolate sauce that instantly hardens when it hits your ice cream).

THE PROCESS

The FDM process falls in the squeezer category. SLA and SLS processes are hardeners. (Reminder: fused deposition modeling, FDM, is also known as fused filament fabrication, FFF, when the process is used by a non-Stratasys company.) FDM uses strands of brightly colored thermoplastic filaments coiled around spools like thick thread. The printer melts the filaments strand by strand, and the nozzle deposits, or squeezes, the melted filament onto the printer

Like cooking, 3D printing relies on a set of instructions to create a final product using specific materials and tools. And like cooking, it is something you can do at home.

platform layer by layer to build the object. Engineers, designers, and hobbyists use FFF for a variety of purposes, including prototypes and finished products. Other squeezer printers include laminated object manufacturing (LOM), bioprinters, and printers of electronics.

SLA relies on a vat of resin, a syrup-like liquid. The printer's UV laser cures, or hardens, the resin, one layer at a time, into a specific shape. The curing is somewhat like flash freezing syrup. The shape appears to emerge from the vat of resin. Engineers and other professionals use SLA to create finished products as well as prototypes in a variety of fields, including aerospace, automotive, medicine, dentistry, arts and entertainment, culinary, architecture, and energy.

SLS requires a vat of powder, something like a tub of fine sand. High-powered lasers melt the powdered particles together. They then form a hardened, solid mass. With SLS, you actually pull your creation out of the remaining powder as if you were pulling a toy out of sand at the beach. Engineers and designers use SLS to create objects with complex shapes and highly durable parts and molds in plastic, ceramic, glass, and metal. SLS works for a variety of fields including aerospace and engineering. Other hardener printers include digital light processing (DLP) and selective laser melting (SLM).

MULTI JET FUSION

In the early twenty-first century, several creators of ink-jet printers—the types of printers we use to print words or images on a page—have also developed new 3D printing processes. In 2014, along with its ink-jet printers, HP revealed its new 3D printing process, called multi jet fusion. Industry reports, along with HP, claim that the multi jet fusion technology works ten times faster than the fastest 3D printers.

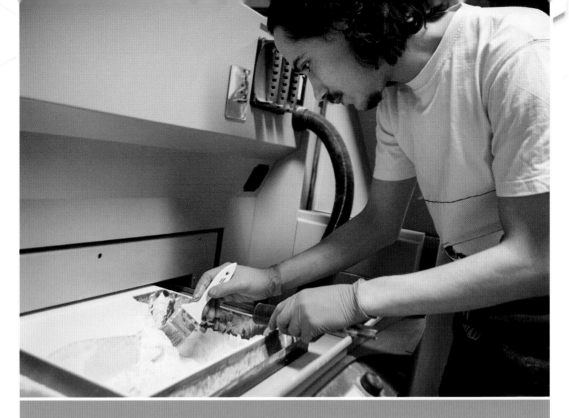

SLS technology 3D prints objects in a bed of powdered material. A laser beam sinters (heats) or melts certain areas of the powder to build the object layer by layer. As it is printed, the rest of the powder supports the piece. Manufacturers then use an air nozzle, a sand blaster, or a simple brush to remove the powder support when the piece is finished.

Multi jet fusion also falls in the hardener category. First, the printer deposits a layer of material onto a platform. Then it drops additional material at thirty million drops per second to build the object, layer by layer. In some cases, the printer builds multiple objects at a time. Finally, it fuses the materials and then heats and cools the object exactly where it needs to make a smooth-edged, well-defined object.

HP provides this technology to aerospace, automotive, medical, dental, life sciences, and a variety of other industries. What material can you use? HP says anything. Companies work

FDM printing uses plastic filaments such as these. Specialty or composite 3D printer filaments combine thermoplastics with metal powder, carbon fiber, wood, and glow-in-the-dark compounds to create hybrid materials for printing.

with HP to print their materials, including electronic, multi-material, and multicolor structures.

THE MATERIALS

The three most common 3D-printed materials are thermoplastic filaments, UV curable resins, and anything that can be made into a powder (metal, ceramic, or plastics). As 3D printing becomes more common, people want to use a wider variety of materials. These include metal and plastic combinations, carbon-fiber and plastic composites, clay, plants, human cells, and even chocolate to name just a few. And 3D technology can use recycled materials. Organizations such as ProtoPrint, the Plastic Bank, and the Perpetual Plastic Project collect and convert plastic waste (such as milk jugs and water bottles) into 3D printer filament. Or you can recycle your 3D plastics with products such as ReDeTec's ProtoCycler. Meanwhile, innovators are looking for more ways to recycle materials other than plastic for 3D printing.

THE HARDWARE

The 3D printers that you'll find in industrial settings are usually large and expensive. They cost about $100,000 to more than $1 million. Smaller, more affordable printers for home or office cost about $1,000, sometimes more. The 3D printing industry began with the larger industrial printers for manufacturers.

The size of the printer determines the size of what you can print. So the geometric shape of the object can't be larger than the 3D printer itself. If it is, you'll need to find a larger printer or do multiple print jobs and then assemble the printed parts. The maximum length, depth, and height that the printer can print is called the build volume. The build volume is expanding as innovators come up with new ideas. For example, robot printers, such as Arevo Labs's Robotic Additive Manufacturing Platform (RAMP), released in 2015, can print anywhere, any size. For engineers, RAMP offers more design possibilities and larger sizes for printed objects because the robot is not limited to the dimensions of a conventional 3D printer.

Autodesk and other companies are experimenting with 3D printing systems that use multiple printing heads to help a manufacturer make a large object in one print job. Autodesk is working on the software for this hardware in hopes that manufacturers of 3D printers for engineers, professionals, and the home market will jump on board to build these multiple-printhead printers. The software breaks up large designs into multiple sets of instructions that can then be sent to multiple printheads simultaneously. The benefits to this approach include printing larger objects, taking less time to print small objects, and doing multiple jobs at once by swapping out printheads for other tools. A robotic hand, for example, could help the printer by repositioning parts of the object being printed to allow the printer to continue printing.

THE SOFTWARE

The software for 3D printing started with CAD tools that required advanced engineering skills to use. In the twenty-first century,

With CAD software, users can design just about anything for 3D printing. The hardware fits easily on a desk or tabletop.

anyone with a computer can use CAD, freeform modeling, sculpting, and 3D immersive design tools. CAD tools such as SketchUp and Tinkercad use geometric shapes to build 3D models. Freeform modeling tools allow designers to create many different shapes. Anything you can draw, you could potentially 3D print using freeform modeling software such as 123D Creature or Blender. Sculpting tools work like clay, allowing a designer to push, pull, pinch, and grab elements to form 3D models digitally. Sculpting software includes 123D Sculpt and Leopoly. Immersive design tools include software and hardware that combine 3D scanning, modeling, and printing to move between reality and digital 3D worlds almost seamlessly. One popular immersive tool is HP Sprout.

You can play with many of these software tools for free. Check out resources such as the 3D Printing for Beginners website for descriptions and links to download the software. The more you play, the more you can add your voice, innovations, and skills to the 3D manufacturing revolution.

THE FILE FORMATS

3D PRINTING RELIES ON FOUR MAIN FILE FORMATS:

STL. Innovator Chuck Hull created the STL file format, the oldest, most common 3D file type. It interfaces between (talks to) 3D software and 3D printers. STL was created to handle simple one-color, one-material objects for prototypes, not finished products. STL does not handle more complex print jobs that require multiple colors or multiple materials.

OBJ. Object file is a common file format for 3D printing. Many design software programs allow you to save files in OBJ, and most printers accept OBJ as a printable file.

AMF. The additive manufacturing file format allows any design software to describe the shape and composition of any object to be printed on any 3D printer. The international ASTM Committee F42 on Additive Manufacturing Technologies developed the format, hoping it will become the standard for 3D printing file format.

3MF. 3D Manufacturing Format is a Microsoft Windows format. It is becoming more common for 3D printing. Microsoft wants 3MF to become the standard.

CHAPTER 3

3D PRINTING AND TRADITIONAL MANUFACTURING

Additive manufacturing, also known as 3D printing, is actually more of a manufacturing process than a printing process. Adding materials layer by layer to create an object is part of what makes 3D printing revolutionary. In contrast to 3D printing, traditional manufacturing subtracts or removes materials to make a product—an object is cut from or built from other materials. Building a house, for example, involves first cutting down and then chopping up trees, creating boards at a lumberyard, and then moving them to a construction site, where workers build the house. This process can be wasteful. It doesn't use all the processed wood. And it uses a lot of fuel to get workers and materials to a site. Wood is just one of many traditional manufacturing materials. Other materials—such as nails, glues, drywall, bricks, stone, and flooring—also have to be produced and shipped, often to or from many different places around the globe. But by 3D printing a house, local materials can be used with very little waste at the site. A 3D-printed home is built with

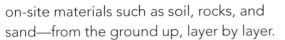

on-site materials such as soil, rocks, and sand—from the ground up, layer by layer.

Traditional manufacturing excels at mass production—making many of one thing, all exactly alike. In contrast, 3D printing excels at mass customization. This model of production starts with a basic design that can be changed digitally to make many objects, each one unique to an individual person. The object could be a new cell phone that you design, invisible braces that fit your mouth exactly, or shoes that are a perfect match for your feet and your style.

Manufacturers, professionals, and anyone who wants to can use 3D printing to customize objects for their customers and for their own use. As a business or hobby, 3D printing can work in these ways:

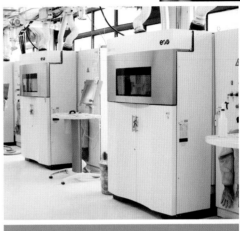

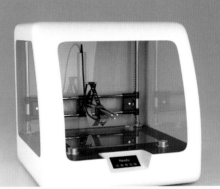

3D printers can be as big as the printers (*top*) at the Shapeways production headquarters in New York or as small as this tabletop model (*above*).

1. **Businesses print for other businesses.** Manufacturers can provide prototypes, molds, final products, or 3D printing services to other businesses. For example, an aerospace company that uses 3D print molds to create airplane engine parts may sell the molds to an airplane manufacturer to build airplanes.

2. **Businesses print for themselves.** Manufacturers 3D print their own prototypes, molds, or final products for their own

REPRAP

Imagine a 3D printer that prints several 3D printers. Those printers then print another batch of 3D printers. And so on. In 2005 British engineer-mathematician Adrian Bowyer invented exactly that. A printer—the RepRap printer—that prints itself.

Before he even knew about 3D printing, Bowyer had dreamed of making a machine that could replicate itself. When the University of Bath, where he taught in England, received a grant that allowed the university to buy several 3D printers, Bowyer got two. The more he worked with the printers, the more he saw the potential of 3D printers to print themselves. And Bowyer realized that for 3D printing to be something that everyone could use, it would have to be a technology that consumers could use easily and freely. So, when he made the RepRap 3D printer, he made sure that all RepRap designs and creations are open source—or free to the public. This means anyone can use them and copy them. The cost of a RepRap printer? About $200.

businesses. For example, an automobile company could 3D print prototypes for its innovative car designs.

3. **Businesses print for consumers.** Companies can provide 3D printing services or final products to customers. For example, a company may 3D print jewelry or orthodontic braces that are ready to purchase and wear.

4. **Individuals, often hobbyists or do-it-yourself makers, 3D print for themselves.** They may design their items or pay someone to do it. They may print objects at home or pick up the item at a 3D printing service center near them. For example, you may decide to 3D print custom toys for yourself or your friends or print kitchen gadgets for your parents.

3D PRINTING AND PERSONAL MANUFACTURING

Bre Pettis, Adam Mayer, and Zach "Hoeken" Smith founded MakerBot in Brooklyn, New York, in January 2009. The MakerBot trio believed in the RepRap vision: a 3D printer that could print itself. They felt

MakerBot founders (*left to right*) Adam Mayer, Zach Smith, and Bre Pettis with the final prototypes of their MakerBot Cupcake printer. The inventors' goal was to make small, affordable 3D printers that people could use at home.

that everyone who wanted one should have a 3D printer and that the printers should be open source. That is, the software and hardware designs can be used by anyone, without charge, and with the ability to change and share ideas and designs freely.

Hobbyists and makers devoured the original MakerBot printers, with family-friendly names such as Cupcake, Thing-o-matic, and Replicator. In 2013 Stratasys bought MakerBot. MakerBot runs as a separate division of Stratasys, continuing to make desktop 3D printing for professional, educational, and home use. None of the original founders are part of MakerBot or Stratasys.

MakerBot printers use FFF technology and filaments. They use acrylonitrile butadiene styrene (ABS), the same plastic that Lego blocks are made of. The printers also use polylactic acid (PLA), a biodegradable plastic made of starch from corn, potatoes, grains, and beets.

As 3D printers continue to become more sophisticated and affordable, more people have 3D tools that previously were only available to large industrial manufacturers. For example, SLA technology was once far too expensive and difficult for most people to use. Yet SLA provides more accurate and higher-resolution 3D printing and with a smoother finish than FFF does. MakerBot offers FFF as a more affordable technology. In 2012 MIT graduate students Max Lobovsky, Nathan Linder, and David Cranor set out to change things. They wanted professionals in engineering, medicine, dentistry, art, clothing, and jewelry to be able to buy affordable SLA 3D printers that work in the home or office.

> ❝ SOME PEOPLE THINK THAT A 3D PRINTER CAN MAKE ANYTHING. NOT TRUE. EACH TYPE OF 3D PRINTER DOES A SPECIFIC TYPE OF JOB. YOU NEED THE RIGHT TOOL FOR THE JOB.❞
>
> —Max Lobovsky, cofounder and CEO, Formlabs

FORMLABS

Max Lobovsky started his quest for the right tool for any job by playing with machines as a kid. Lots of machines: robots, 3D printers, milling machines, computers, electronic components, and programming tools, to name a few. In 1993, when he was six years old, Max started playing with and learning about machines from his parents, who are engineers from the Ukraine. Growing up in New Jersey, Max participated in FIRST (For Inspiration and Recognition of Science and Technology) Robotics competitions. He continued playing with machines at Cornell University in New York and at graduate school at MIT. Along the way, he met other people who liked to play with machines too.

In graduate school, Lobovsky focused on designing robots at MIT Media Lab. This lab on the MIT campus is a unique place to learn and create. It encourages unconventional mixing and matching of disciplines and research. Students and faculty collaborate on multiple teams to explore, learn, and pioneer new technologies. Some well-known MIT Media Lab products include Scratch, a free programming language that helps users create their own stories, games, and animations. Lego Mindstorms is another Media Lab creation. It is a programmable robotics construction set that enables users to build, program, and command their own Lego robots.

Meanwhile, Lobovsky also helped set up Fab Labs across the United States. A Fab Lab is a center where all community members can learn and invent new things for free. Each center is equipped with machines and open-source software and programs written by researchers at MIT's Center for Bits and Atoms. All Fab Labs include a laser cutter that makes 2D and 3D structures, a sign cutter that uses copper to make antennas and circuits, and a milling

FIRST ROBOTICS

FIRST Robotics Competition is an international high school robotics competition run by a nonprofit called FIRST. Each year, teams of high school students from around the world work with adult mentors from technical and nontechnical fields. During the school year, they build and program robots to perform challenging tasks. At the competition in April in Houston, Texas, or Saint Louis, Missouri, each team demonstrates what its robot can do. As part of the competition, each team must also develop a business plan, design a team brand, hone teamwork skills, and perform community outreach as part of the design challenge.

In 2016, the twenty-fifth year of competition, 3,140 teams with about 78,500 students and 19,000 mentors from twenty-four countries built robots. They competed in fifty-three regional competitions, sixty-five district qualifying competitions, and eight district championships. Six hundred teams won slots to attend the FIRST Championship, where they competed in a tournament. Winners were then chosen from a variety of categories. But the main goal of the competition isn't winning. It's about learning valuable engineering and team-building skills.

Formlabs founder Max Lobovsky speaks at a session in 2014 at the South by Southwest (SXSW) Music, Film, and Interactive Conference and Festival in Austin, Texas. The event celebrates music and film as well as emerging technologies. The documentary film *Print the Legend* came out that year, highlighting 3D printing technologies and innovators such as Lobovsky.

machine that makes circuit boards and precision parts. The labs also have a large wood router for building furniture and housing, and they have electronic components and programming tools. Fab Labs help people learn and mentor one another. Participants gain deep knowledge about the machines, materials, design, and engineering that go into invention and innovation.

When Lobovsky was finishing his graduate degree in media arts and sciences at MIT, he thought a lot about what to do next. He says, "I noticed that a couple of companies had started up, including MakerBot, to make commercial desktop 3D printers. I looked at what was out there [for 3D printing]. It was exciting, but I thought it was possible to make something better. There were about six types of 3D printers at the time and only FDM was available for desktop 3D printing." Max wondered, "Why can't we have more 3D printing tools for the desktop? Why can't we have high-resolution 3D printing at low cost for the desktop?"

These questions inspired Lobovsky to start his own company, Formlabs, in 2012. "I got together with two other students at MIT, Nathan Linder and David Cranor. We raised some money and started building the Form 1 printer," Lobovsky remembers. He and his friends launched Formlabs with a record-breaking $3 million Kickstarter campaign.

Formlabs created a 3D printing system of hardware, software, materials, and process that allows professionals to produce high-quality 3D products with SLA technology. "Whether you are an artist, architect, dentist, engineer, or jeweler, you should be able to use a 3D printer like an office printer. You don't need to worry about how it works. If you know the software and can design what you want, you can print it," Lobovsky says.

A month after Formlabs raised the money on Kickstarter, Chuck Hull's 3D Systems sued Formlabs for patent infringement. Hull's company

KICKSTARTER

Kickstarter is an online fund-raising community. Anyone (designers, artists, and developers) can pitch an idea for a creative project. Anyone can fund it and follow its success. Kickstarter projects range from movies to video games and from band performances to portable high-quality sound systems. Innovators have raised as little as a few thousand dollars over a few weeks to millions of dollars in a couple of days—and everything in between.

Famous Kickstarter success stories include Palo Alto, California–based smartwatch maker Pebble. It got its start with a record-breaking Kickstarter campaign in 2012. In 2015 Pebble beat its own record—and everyone else's—by raising $20,338,986 for the Pebble Time watch. The *Veronica Mars* Movie Project, based on the Veronica Mars cult TV series (2004–2007) is a Kickstarter success too. The TV show starred Kristin Bell as a teenage private investigator, and with support from the fans known as Marshmallows, the project raised $5,702,153. The film was released in theaters on March 14, 2014.

didn't think Formlabs had the legal right to use SLA in its 3D printers and sell them. Faced with a lawsuit like this, some people would have given up or spent all their time dealing with the lawsuit. Not Lobovsky and his team. They got busy addressing the lawsuit *and* building their business. They knew they couldn't ignore 3D Systems, but they also knew that they couldn't let the lawsuit stop them.

It took Formlabs eight months to get the first Form 1 printer out the door and two years to settle the lawsuit. It took teamwork to make both things happen. Lobovsky says, "Collaboration is key. You need to get together a really great team of people to build something like this. That's where I spend most of my time now—building the team."

> ## " COLLABORATION IS KEY. YOU NEED TO GET TOGETHER A REALLY GREAT TEAM OF PEOPLE TO BUILD SOMETHING LIKE THIS. THAT'S WHERE I SPEND MOST OF MY TIME NOW—BUILDING THE TEAM."
>
> **—Max Lobovsky, cofounder and CEO, Formlabs**

NADIA

Remember that FIRST Robotics program? Six of the first ten hires at Formlabs competed in FIRST Robotics. Lobovsky met his wife, Nadia Cheng, at a robotics summer camp. Later, Cheng helped build Formlabs. Lobovsky explains, "Nadia was basically a volunteer part time employee with all kinds of odd tasks: helping with pitch presentations, designing demo parts, building prototypes with us." With a doctorate in mechanical engineering from MIT, Cheng's interests and work include robotics and personal fabrication technologies, such as the 3D-printed products made possible by Formlabs.

Cheng directs research and development at a robotics company, and she is still involved with Formlabs. Cheng uses Formlabs printers to create prototypes of robotic components such as intricate chambers that can't be built using traditional manufacturing. She also creates prototypes for robotic fingers. Yes, fingers. Formlabs resins include tough yet flexible materials to print robot hands with movable joints. Cheng says, "It's awesome that we can print out the [robot's] flexible fingers for prototyping." Lobovsky says, "Nadia has used all of our products extensively in her work, so she is one of our greatest sources of customer feedback and testing."

CHAPTER 4
3D PRINTING OUR HEALTH

How many things have you touched today that were 3D printed? With a growing number of 3D manufacturers, the answer is a lot. More than 70 percent of manufacturers have adopted 3D printing, using it mostly for developing prototypes and for creating final products. More than 50 percent of manufacturers expect they will use 3D printing for high-volume production in the next three to five years. Traditional manufacturers are not the only ones using 3D printers. About 85 percent of the half million 3D printers that have been ordered and shipped are going to users of personal desktop 3D printers. So individuals and small businesses are 3D printing too.

Although 3D printing started as a technique for prototyping for traditional manufacturing, it has grown into a revolution that is changing how average people make and get what they need. It touches our basic needs in medical care, food, and clothing. And 3D printing is part of our play and travel as well. We can print our own electronic gadgets and toys, as well as key parts for Earth and space travel.

Here are the areas in which 3D printing is having the most impact:

MEDICINE

The 3D revolution in medicine so far includes 3D-printed prosthetic devices (also known as prostheses), prototypes, and bioprinting.

PROSTHETICS

Several organizations, such as E-nable, Nia Technologies, and Not Impossible, provide inexpensive, easy-to-develop 3D-printed prostheses, or artificial limbs. Printed prostheses are life changing. And since children quickly outgrow their prosthetic devices, 3D printing brings down the cost of replacing the devices as young people grow. Some adults, who cannot afford a traditionally manufactured prosthesis, may prefer a more affordable 3D-printed model. The National Institutes of Health (NIH) 3D Print Exchange has an

Orthopedic technology specialist Moses Kaweesa works on a 3D-printed artificial limb socket at the CoRSU Rehabilitation Hospital in Uganda. With an infrared scanner, a laptop, and a pair of 3D printers, he can make the sockets in a day rather than a week. And they are more comfortable than traditionally manufactured sockets.

online collection of scientifically accurate 3D printable prosthetics. The exchange also includes modeling tutorials and educational materials. The designs are organized by E-nable online so that anyone—engineers as well as the general public—can download and print the designs for free.

Other organizations seek to make prosthetics more comfortable and more functional. For example, in the civil war (1991–2002) in Sierra Leone, Africa, rebel forces amputated limbs of more than eight thousand men, women, and children as part of a fear campaign. Most amputees did not wear their prosthetic devices because they were so uncomfortable. The devices rub against skin and can cause sores and rashes. Growing up in Sierra Leone, David Sengeh saw thousands of people in his country struggling to wear their prosthetics. He wanted to make a difference. While a graduate student at MIT from 2010 to 2015, he 3D printed prosthetic sockets so that the connection between the mechanical parts of the prosthetic and the amputee's skin fit comfortably. The sockets can be produced cheaply and quickly. And more people are likely to wear their prosthetics because they are more comfortable. Sengeh is an entrepreneur and the president of the board for Global Minimum. This organization raises money to make innovations such as 3D-printed prosthetic sockets a reality.

Superhero Cyborgs is a group for young people aged ten to fifteen who live with a disability. They make their own souped-up prosthetics to have fun, solve problems, and learn 3D printing skills. They work with designers and engineers to design and 3D print prosthetics that can do anything. For example, the group has made prosthetics that spray water, lift weights, or work like a Swiss army knife. One prosthetic even fits multiple attachments.

PROTOTYPE HEARTS

Doctors and medical researchers use 3D printing to create lifesaving prototypes. For example, each year, about forty thousand babies are born with a congenital heart defect in the United States. Many of these babies will have to have surgery.

Because they grow over time, the babies often have to have multiple surgeries. Doctors have tools to tell them what is wrong with a child's heart. But they can't actually examine the heart from every angle or look inside it until the surgery begins. A 3D model of a patient's heart changes everything, says pediatric cardiologist Dr. Matthew Bramlet at OSF Saint Francis Medical Center in Peoria, Illinois. A surgeon can examine the exterior and interior of the 3D-printed heart, which looks just like the patient's real heart.

Bramlet learned of this technology in 2010 at a medical institution in Toronto, Ontario. There, doctors put magnetic resonance imaging (MRI) of a heart into a CAD program and then 3D printed the heart out of plastic. Bramlet tested the technology on a 3D printer at the Jump Trading Simulation and Education Center on the OSF Saint Francis campus. The cost of the technology is low, about $20 for a 3D-printed heart. Building a model of a patient's heart using traditional techniques would cost $6,000.

Dr. Shi-Joon Yoo, at the Hospital for Sick Children in Toronto, helped develop these 3D-printed models of toddler hearts. The models were based on the hearts of real patients. With them, surgeons can practice and prepare for rare and difficult cases.

Trial runs of 3D-printed hearts showed the value of the technique to surgeons. Luke Snodgrass and his family know the benefits of this technology firsthand. Luke was born with a congenital heart defect. He had an operation when he was six months old and needed another when he was three. His doctors planned the surgery to reconstruct Luke's heart. However, the surgery would leave him with one instead of two ventricles. (These organs of the heart pump blood to the lungs and the rest of the body.) Even with this plan, Luke would eventually need a heart transplant.

Luke's parents went to Bramlet for a second opinion. At first, he and his colleagues agreed with Luke's doctors. Then they did MRIs of Luke's heart so they could 3D print a model. From looking at the 3D model, they found that they could take a different approach. In a different type of surgery, the surgeon would place a pacemaker (to control heart rhythms) in Luke's diaphragm (under the lungs). This would allow Luke to keep both ventricles. Luke's family chose to proceed that way, and the surgery was successful. Luke can run and play like most kids. He will need another surgery when he is older to move his pacemaker to the more traditional shoulder area. But that's it. Doctors have no other surgeries planned for Luke.

Bramlet and his colleagues have built an online database of the best images of heart defects so that other doctors can use them for 3D printing. The database is available from the NIH 3D Print Exchange. These 3D images and printable 3D models give doctors the information they need to repair patients' hearts so they can live full lives.

PROTOTYPE EMERGENCY MASK PODS

Adults are not the only ones making prototypes to solve important health-related challenges. At the age of thirteen, Alexis Lewis read a news story about a mother throwing her baby from a window to escape a fire. Lewis wondered if she

When she was thirteen, Alexis Lewis invented and 3D printed the emergency lifesaving kit she is holding. It is lightweight and easy to use. Lewis stays current on new technologies by reading magazines such as *New Scientist*, *Discover*, *Wired*, and *Popular Science* cover to cover.

could create lifesaving supplies that emergency professionals and neighbors could throw into windows of burning buildings to save the people inside. She could and she did. She invented the patented Emergency Mask Pod, a kit of lifesaving supplies.

In 2013 Lewis used Tinkercad (a free online CAD program) and a MakerBot Replicator 2 3D printer to develop several different prototypes for the projectile (throwable) pods. To test the pods, thirty-seven firefighters threw each prototype into a second-story window more than 290 times. A football-shaped pod was the clear winner, with an accuracy rate of more than 70 percent.

The Emergency Mask Pod has a small strip on the outside that lights up. Inside the pod is a smoke mask made by Xcaper Industries and a pair of eye goggles. The goggles help protect people's eyes from burning. The mask makes it easier for people to breathe in a smoke-filled room. The light strip helps people find the pod in a dark, smoky room.

BIOPRINTING

For more than a decade, researchers have experimented with the lifesaving potential of bioprinting—printing with living cells as the material. Bioprinters have successfully made human ears, noses, skull bones, jawbones, bladders, and other body parts. Surgeons have placed these 3D-printed body parts into patients successfully. Some of these bioprinted parts are designed so that the body will eventually absorb them.

That's what happened to Kaiba Gionfriddo. He was born in 2012 in Youngstown, Ohio, with a condition that prevented him from breathing normally. He was diagnosed with tracheobronchomalacia. His trachea (windpipe)—the organ that enables a person to breathe and speak—was so weak that it collapsed. In the past, babies with this condition did not live long.

In Kaiba's case, doctors performed a surgery called a tracheostomy to strengthen the trachea. Even after the surgery, Kaiba would frequently stop breathing. Without oxygen, his heart would stop too. His parents learned that doctors at the University of Michigan had developed a 3D-printed bioabsorbable stent for conditions like Kaiba's.

In medicine, a stent is a device inserted into a tubular area, such as a blood vessel or trachea. The stent expands the tube to

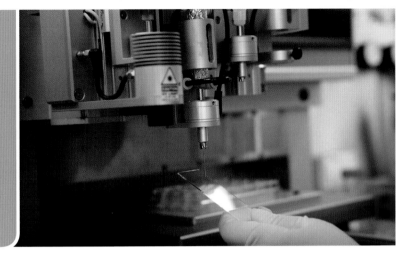

The printheads of 3D bioprinters are like syringes. They quickly and very precisely place living cells and other materials into dishes, tubes, or other medical platforms. Bioprinters cost anywhere from $10,000 to $200,000.

prevent or lessen blockage. Traditionally, such devices are made from metal mesh and remain in the body permanently or until a doctor removes them surgically. A bioabsorbable stent serves the same purpose. However, it is manufactured from a material that dissolves or is absorbed in the body so no additional surgeries are needed to remove the stent.

Kaiba's team took computerized tomography (CT) scans of his trachea, created a 3D model on the computer, and printed it with a laser-based 3D printer. Surgeons placed the new stent into Kaiba's trachea to open his airway. The surgery was successful, and Kaiba breathes normally and leads an active, healthy life.

DRUGS

Have you ever gotten a pill caught in your throat? One of those big chalky ones that just doesn't seem to go down no matter how much water you swallow? A 3D printer can help. Aprecia Pharmaceuticals designed a 3D-printed drug, called Spritam, for people who take medications to manage epileptic seizures. It's the first drug in a line of 3D-printed drugs this company plans to create, print, and sell to consumers.

Aprecia calls the 3D-printed pills fast-melts because they are porous (allow water to pass through) and therefore melt in the mouth. The company can even customize the pills to a patient's condition and body size. With a mathematical algorithm, the company can determine the right dosage for each person. Aprecia Pharmaceuticals has a specific 3D printing technology, called the ZipDose Technology platform, which the company patented to make Spritam and other 3D-printed drugs.

In the United States, the US Food and Drug Administration (FDA) approves new pharmaceutical drugs and new techniques for making them before they are sold. The FDA has approved the technique for making the first 3D-printed drugs, but many Americans have questions. How do pharmacists and consumers get access to a ZipDose printer? Legally, who is responsible if the drug causes harm? Is it the organization that made the printer, the provider of the ingredients for the pill, the creator of the algorithm for the pill, or the individual or organization that printed it? These questions are unanswered, and the FDA will grapple with them as they review 3D-printed drugs.

DENTISTRY

You may not think of a trip to the dentist as a revolutionary experience, but it soon may be. Dentists use 3D printers to print the tools that guide them during oral surgeries. They also print invisible aligners (braces) to align teeth and retainers to keep that alignment in place. They also print crowns, a type of replacement tooth. What used to take months and several appointments with a dentist may soon be done in minutes at one appointment.

A college student named Amos Dudley had an amazing idea. He showed all of us, including the dental industry, just how revolutionary 3D-printed dentistry can be.

Dentists can use 3D printing to make a range of dental products. Improved technology has increased the speed of printing so a dentist can print a new tooth in a matter of minutes.

DIY DENTISTRY

In college at the New Jersey Institute of Technology, Amos Dudley realized he wasn't smiling much. He wasn't unhappy. He just didn't like the way his teeth looked. He had had braces in high school. But like many people, he stopped wearing his retainer, and his teeth moved out of alignment. He couldn't afford to pay $8,000 for another round of braces so he decided to take matters into his own hands—and to a 3D printer. He researched clear orthodontic (tooth) alignment technology and discovered that dental professionals 3D print the invisible liners. He wondered if he could 3D print his own liners, as a do-it-yourself dentistry project.

Dudley quickly realized he needed to know more than how to print the liners. He needed to know what it takes to align your own teeth. Dudley remembers, "[I needed] knowledge of orthodontic movement, a 3D scanner, a mold of the teeth, CAD software, a hi-res 3D printer, retainer material, and a vacuum-forming machine." He realized he had access to all of these things. However, the dimensional accuracy of his 3D printer wasn't good enough. His college has a digital fabrication lab with a Stratasys Dimension 1200es 3D printer. The lab allowed him to use the printer for his project. So in 2015, he made it happen.

Caution! Do not do your own dental work. Self-dentistry can go terribly wrong and lead to life-threatening infections and other complications. Dudley did extensive research—and was very lucky. While 3D printing is a powerful tool, use it cautiously and wisely, and always with adult supervision.

THE STEPS DUDLEY TOOK

Step 1: Dudley created an alginate mold of his teeth. Alginate is a wet claylike substance made of seaweed and used by dental professionals.

Step 2: He made a cast. He says, "I put the mold upside down in a yogurt container and then filled it with liquid Permastone, a cast-making material." When the mold was set, he broke off the top to reveal the casting and used a razor blade to smooth out the surrounding area. He added two small colored dots to the surface of the casting. They would serve as reference points to preserve the scale of the mold as he manipulated it digitally.

Step 3: Dudley then scanned the cast with a 3D laser scanner into CAD software. (The 3D laser scanner turns a physical object into a digital object.) He used the CAD software to figure out how much the teeth would need to move to be in alignment. He also figured out how many 3D aligner models he would need to achieve that movement.

Step 4: He used the Stratasys Dimension 1200es to print the 3D models and build a platform.

Step 5: From a seller on eBay, he bought nontoxic thermoplastic made specially for retainers. He used a vacuum-forming process to shape the plastic onto each 3D aligner model.

Step 6: Finally, he removed the vacuum-formed plastic aligners from each 3D-printed model. He used a Dremel tool to smooth the edges so they wouldn't poke his mouth, and he was ready to go.

In 2016 Formlabs engineers saw Dudley's 3D DIY dentistry project on his blog. CEO Max Lobovsky said, "We all saw his post about his DIY dentistry and loved it so I called him up." Dudley accepted the offer to work for Formlabs and went on to become an applications engineer with the company.

CHAPTER 5

3D PRINTING OUR WORLD

Amazing options in health care are available with 3D printing. It is also revolutionizing many other fields, including food, fashion, the arts, archaeology, entertainment, transportation, electronics, and space exploration.

FOOD

The ChefJet, Foodini, and Magic Candy Factory sound like fun alternatives to the Easy-Bake Oven you may have played with as a kid. At this point, 3D food printers are only for chefs to play with as they make high-end culinary creations. Chefs say they like 3D printers because they allow for a whole new level of creativity that's not possible with traditional cooking.

For example, chefs and event planners are using 3D printers to create edible masterpieces. Multicolored sweets in intricate geometric designs can be created by layering sugar that contains all these flavors: vanilla, mint, sour apple, watermelon, and cherry. South Carolina-based 3D Systems makes the ChefJet, whose printhead deposits the sugar material onto a platform, then sprays water onto the sugar. The water creates crystals that eventually harden. If you've ever put water on cake frosting to make a cake glossy, you know that water naturally hardens the sugar. That's the same technique the 3D printer uses, building up these creative candies layer by layer.

Desserts are not the only thing on the 3D menu. Paco Perez at La Enoteca restaurant in Barcelona, Spain, uses Natural Machines' Foodini 3D printer to make his main course creation: Sea Coral. He places a plate inside a machine that looks like a large microwave oven. He touches the controls, and a few minutes later, he removes the plate, which is decorated with a delicate, flowerlike design, created with the layer-by-layer technique using a mix of vegetables. On top of the design, he adds caviar, sea urchins, hollandaise sauce, and foam made from carrots. The centerpiece of the dish, the coral, is an intricate design of seafood puree. The puree design would be extremely difficult to produce by hand. But

The ChefJet 3D printer uses sugar and water to print edible, flavored sweets. The printer costs between $5,000 and $10,000, so it is used mostly in hotels and restaurants, which can afford the high price tag. The ChefJet comes with a digital cookbook to help users design 3D-printed candies.

Perez uses a 3D printer to upload the design and then pipe out the puree onto the plate. "It's very interesting what . . . technology is contributing to gastronomy [the art of cooking]," Perez says. "Creativity is shaped by what technology can do."

In many ways, a 3D printer becomes an assistant chef by automating difficult and repetitive tasks. Lynette Kucsma is a cofounder of Barcelona-based Natural Machines, which makes 3D food printers. She explains, "Imagine you need to print breadsticks in the shape of tree branches for a hundred people. . . . Rather than food piping it . . . you can automate it with a 3D food printer."

A wide range of semisolid food such as mashed potatoes, chocolate, and other purees can be printed with a 3D printer. They are useful in nursing homes, where many older people often have trouble chewing and swallowing solid foods and eat soft foods instead. But they prefer the look and taste of solid foods. 3D food printers can print semisolid foods that are more appealing, in the shape of chicken legs and other foods.

3D printers belong to the world of the Internet of Things. This is a world of interconnected smart devices. They are each equipped with software, sensors, and connection to the Internet. The smart devices exchange information and include everyday items such as smart vacuum cleaners and smart washing machines. And with a smart 3D printer, you can upload recipes and designs to the device from anywhere. These 3D printers do not actually cook yet, but that's coming.

CLOTHING

Make your own clothes with a click of a button. No needle or thread required. With 3D-printed clothes and shoes, you can show off your fashion design and technology skills. For example, Electroloom was a company that developed the Electroloom 3D fabric printer and companion fabrics for people to create their own custom seamless clothing. The company, based in San Francisco, California, worked with customers to create 3D molds for designs using a CAD program. Each mold could be reused or

Israeli fashion designer Noa Raviv lives and works in New York. She created these 3D-printed black-and-white dresses when she was twenty-eight. They were part of a summer 2016 exhibit called Manus x Machina: Fashion in an Age of Technology at the Costume Institute of the Metropolitan Museum of Art in New York City.

remolded for the next fashion creation. The company folded in 2016, but innovators continue to develop the technology.

Once the mold is ready, you place it in the 3D printer chamber. The fabric comes in a liquid solution made of various fibers, both natural and synthetic, and in a variety of colors. The fiber solution goes into the printer. The printer guides the solution onto the mold using an electric field that binds the fibers together into a solid, seamless fabric in the shape of the mold. The Electroloom printer looked a bit like the *Star Trek* transporter. But instead of people materializing, there comes a shirt, skirt, or pair of pants!

If you have a 3D-printed outfit, you may want some shoes too. You can choose to customize your favorite athletic shoes and have them 3D printed for you by companies such as Nike and New Balance. You can also customize and print your own Klöts for your new athletic shoes. Klöts are two interlocking puzzle pieces that keep your shoelaces tight and tidy.

Or if you need something a bit more formal, you can travel over to the Feetz website to customize your shoes. First, you take pictures of your feet using the Feetz app and your smartphone or tablet. Next, you choose the design, colors, and size of the shoes you want. Then you upload your photos and your order to Feetz. Their digital cobblers (shoemakers) use the images you sent to 3D print your shoes. They'll ship your shoes to you. Outfit complete!

ANCIENT ARTIFACTS

Modern 3D-printed food, clothes, and shoes are one thing. But 3D printing is also changing what we know about ancient artifacts and what they tell us about ourselves. Researchers are using pictures of artifacts from all angles and measurements to 3D print models of the artifacts. They can even print a model of the excavation site where an artifact was found. Artifacts and archaeological sites are extremely fragile, so researchers work hard to protect them. They can use 3D models to study artifacts and sites in a way that will not damage or destroy them. And in museums, curators (the experts who bring together a collection of artworks and other interesting objects) use 3D printing too. They create 3D models of delicate pieces for public display. The original piece stays in safekeeping so it will not be harmed by exposure to daylight and humidity. After printing, the original piece can go back to its original owner, if there is one.

The curators of the Smithsonian Institution X 3D project—an effort to make more artifacts available in new ways through 3D printing—have lots of artifacts to work with. The institution's nineteen museums, nine research centers, and National Zoo contain more than 137 million objects, artworks, and living specimens. While they have a long way to go, the X 3D team's goal is to change how we experience artifacts. They want visitors to see more and actually hold artifacts. For example, X 3D uses 3D printing technology to allow visitors to create a working telegraph, a nineteenth-century electrical machine that sent messages over wires.

Researchers have as much fun with 3D-printed artifacts as museum visitors. Billy Ó Foghlú, a researcher at the Australian National University in Canberra, Australia, wondered why there were no ancient bronze horn mouthpieces in Ireland. Ancient horns of many types had been found in Ireland. Mouthpieces have been found all over Europe, but not in Ireland. He began to suspect that the artifact that experts thought was a spear-butt (an end piece of a spear) was actually a mouthpiece for a horn. How could he prove it?

The spear-butt was too fragile to test. Instead, Ó Foghlú obtained its measurements and 3D printed his own copy in bronze. He placed it in the end of a horn from the same historical period and blew. The sound was rich and natural, and the horn was easy to play with the piece in place. He was right. The spear-butt is actually an ancient bronze Irish horn mouthpiece.

Misidentified ancient objects are very common. It's exciting to use 3D-printed objects to investigate how artifacts worked and what their purpose may have been. You, along with researchers, can do the investigating with 3D printing!

TOYS

Have you ever thought about being a toy maker? Toy maker Mattel wants to share that role with consumers with its ThingMaker. Designed for people ages thirteen and up, the Mattel app allows people to design toys on an iPad, phone, or

Toys are easy to 3D print. This PieceMaker Technologies 3D printer kiosk, for example, prints toy pickup trucks. The printer is designed for use in malls and other stores and accepts credit card payment. Printing time is usually thirty minutes or less.

computer. Then you can 3D print the parts and assemble them. You can also use Mattel's designs on whatever 3D printer you like, including Mattel's ThingMaker. Depending on how complex you make your toy, the whole process can take a few minutes or several hours. You can watch your toy print through the glass cover of the ThingMaker printer. The app comes with dozens of basic blueprints (including rings, necklaces, scorpions, dinosaurs, and skeletons). Users can customize toys by color, and they can print new parts.

Other companies such as Shapeways allow customers to design their own custom toys. Then the company 3D prints them and ships them.

ELECTRONICS

Have you thought about 3D printing a cell phone? Or an electronic toy that prints complete with all the electronics inside? The company Voxel8 builds 3D printers that print working devices.

The goal, according to founder and CEO Jennifer Lewis, is to make electronics manufacturing faster, cheaper, more flexible, and more innovative.

The Voxel8 3D printer prints both thermoplastics and conductive inks—inks that can construct wires for electronic components and circuits through which electric pulses pass. The star of this story isn't the 3D printer, it's the materials. The company started with Jennifer Lewis's vision. She was a materials science professor at Harvard University in Massachusetts who "fell in love with the idea of creating matter that matters."

Lewis and her team at Harvard, the Lewis Group, spent more than a decade developing conductive materials that they could squeeze through a printhead onto plastic materials, much like how you squeeze toothpaste onto a toothbrush. Based on their research, the team developed the Voxel8 developer kit in 2016. It includes a 3D printer, conductive printing materials, and software. Industrial designers and engineers from many fields use the kit, for objects large and small. A Voxel8 3D printer may fit on a desktop, for printing small objects. Or the printers may be large enough to print something as large as a Ferris wheel. Voxel8 3D printers can print batteries, sensors, robots, watches, hearing aids, and drones. The quadcopter drone literally flew off the printer, complete with a plastic body and metal circuitry inside.

Lewis envisions a future in which people can print their own computer parts or robotic toys at home. "We ultimately want to mass-customize electronics," she says.

TRANSPORTATION

One day, Richard Hatfield asked himself, "What do I want to be when I grow up?" He loved riding motorcycles and racing cars. He had always believed that an electric vehicle could outlast and outrace a combustion engine vehicle. He decided to prove it with

3D printers can make simple, lightweight drones such as this quadcopter. This type of flying electronic device gets its lift and forward movement from battery-operated rotors, or propellers. Researchers use them in studies to learn more about navigation and flight control. The military and law enforcement use them for camera surveillance. Consumers fly them for fun.

an electric motorcycle. He wanted to 3D print the parts in time for a big race called the Pikes Peak International Hill Climb in July 2013. The yearly race is 12 miles (19 kilometers) long, with a nearly 5,000-foot (1,524 m) climb of Pikes Peak in Pike National Forest, Colorado, to the finish line at the top. And by the way, Hatfield wasn't a teenager or college student when he asked himself the question. He was a successful banker and software developer in his fifties.

He and his Lightning Motorcycle team, based in San Carlos, California, designed and 3D-printed prototypes, lots of prototypes—many times a day, over many years—of different parts of the bike. They used a 3D printer and Autodesk's Dreamcatcher. This goal-directed design (GDD) system enables designers to input design information, including functionality, materials, performance goals, and costs. The software works with the help of cloud computing (an Internet-based system for processing and storing data). It generates graphical designs with lots of details. Many manufacturers of cars and airplanes use similar 3D printing technologies to rapidly print prototype parts, electrical components, and whole cars.

As they experimented, Hatfield's team made step-by-step changes to the bike parts to improve the way the bike would perform. For example, they wanted lightweight parts, reduced drag (resistance), and improved traction. These changes would allow the bike to go as fast and as far as possible. By the time the design was complete, the team had created an electric motorcycle that could go 218 miles (351 km) an hour!

Finally, the day of the big race arrived. The best cars and bikes in the world lined up at the base of the climb. Lightning Motorcycle's bike was there too. Ready to race. Lightning's electric motorcycle finished more than twenty seconds ahead of the competition. In the world of superbikes, that made Lightning Motorcycle an Olympic athlete.

What does this mean off the racetrack? Hatfield says, "The same things that enabled us to build a motorcycle to go 218 mph [351 km] also allow us to build a lighter, more efficient vehicle that goes twice as far with the same amount of energy." This means vehicles of the future will be more energy efficient and use less fuel. This could be an important innovation to help the environment.

APWorks in Taufkirchen, Germany, developed the Light Rider, a 3D-printed electric motorbike. Weighing about 77 pounds (35 kilograms), the Light Rider is about 30 percent lighter than most conventional e-motorcycles, so it can go faster than conventional e-motorcycles. It can go from 0 to 50 miles (0 to 80 km) per hour in seconds, and it can travel almost 37 miles (60 km) between battery charges. APWorks printed the bike on a 3D printer with its trademarked Scalmalloy material. This aluminum alloy (mix of metals) is resistant to corrosion (rust). It is nearly as strong as titanium, a super lightweight, tough material. The key to the Light Rider's light weight is its hollow frame, which is only possible to create using 3D technology.

HASTI AFSARIFARD

Hasti Afsarifard is a twenty-four-year-old woman with a calm and thoughtful passion for the possibilities of 3D printing. She started her 3D quest with her love for building things out of anything. She spent hours building forts with her younger brother when they were both in grade school in Atherton, near San Francisco, California. They used furniture, boxes, stones, dirt—any materials they could find—to build the forts. When she wasn't building, she was coming up with new things to do on the computer. At the age of five, she found a way to make her family's home computer, a computer that did not have Internet access, call her family's home phone. She was pleased. Her father was amazed.

Afsarifard's parents are immigrants from Iran. They met and married in California, and they both influenced her career. Her father is an entrepreneur. He has several restaurants and real estate investment businesses. From him, Afsarifard developed an interest in business. Her mother is a computer engineer. From her, Afsarifard developed an interest in technology. She says, "[My mother] would show us the inside

> " MY DREAM IS TO MAKE 3D PRINTING ACCESSIBLE TO EVERYONE. BY EDUCATING PEOPLE ABOUT IT AND MAKING SURE THEY HAVE ACCESS TO IT. MAYBE NOT IN EVERYONE'S HOME, BUT AT LEAST THEY CAN ACCESS A [3D-PRINTED] PRODUCT IF THEY NEED IT."
>
> —Hasti Afsarifard, 3D printing innovator

of a computer and talk about the parts. Or have us take apart electronics to learn how they worked."

As a teen, Afsarifard learned how to run a business from spending many days with her father at his restaurant in San Francisco. She says, "Both my parents would take us to work with them to show us what they did. We learned a lot." She also continued to build and explore technologies as a teenager. She enjoyed designing on the computer. She learned video production, photo editing, and graphic design. Afsarifard explains, "I like to paint, but I feel that I can express more in the digital work than I can on paper."

3D PRINTING IN COLLEGE

Afsarifard went to college at the University of California, Santa Cruz (UCSC). In 2012, during spring break, her older brother showed her a video of someone digitally designing and 3D printing a drone and flying it. She thought it was interesting. Back at school, she had a class assignment to develop a business plan for a new business. That was when she had an aha moment. "What if everyone had access to 3D printing?" she asked herself. So Afsarifard began reading about 3D printing, taking classes in the community, and meeting 3D printing entrepreneurs. She was hooked. She started telling all her college friends about 3D printing and what it could do. At first, many of them looked at her as if she had just told them that pigs can fly. But soon they started seeing what she was talking about as they read articles and blog posts about 3D printing.

Afsarifard smiles like a teacher pleased with her students when she recalls her friends sharing articles and their excitement about 3D printing with her. "It was great to see my friends so excited. I started looking for opportunities to bring 3D printing to my friends and professors." She met with members of an electrical engineering club who were also interested in 3D printing. She joined the club and, together with other club members, bought a 3D printer, the Ultimaker, for the university's student lab. The club members, including Afsarifard, ran the lab. They advertised their ability to print what people needed using FFF filaments.

The club members did the printing at the lab. They taught faculty and students how to use 3D software to create what they wanted. Afsarifard explains that "many students and faculty wanted simple things, such as phone cases. Others brought their engineering design projects. One engineering student sent her designs for a protective bumper for a drone propeller. Drone propellers often break when they crash into buildings and trees. Propeller replacement can be expensive. The bumper protected the propeller so the drone could keep going even if it bumped into a few walls."

3D PRINTING IN SPACE

One day in Afsarifard's UCSC prototyping class, the teacher talked about several companies using 3D printing technology in new ways. One of the companies caught Afsarifard's attention: Made In Space. This company was founded in 2010 in NASA Ames Research Park in Moffett Field, California. The teacher explained that Made In Space brings 3D printing to astronauts on the International Space Station (ISS). The ISS needs lots of built objects, but it has few resources to build them. If you are in outer space, you can't stop by the local hardware store to find what you need or have FedEx deliver it! As Afsarifard listened, she realized 3D printing could be used for more than just fun. It could have an important purpose.

In 2014 Afsarifard got her bachelor's degree in economics, with a minor in technology and information management. That summer she started working as a summer intern for Made In Space. She remembers, "I was sucked into the [Made In Space] start-up [new company just getting started as a business]! Everything happened quickly. There were about twenty employees. We brainstormed a lot as a group. It was so collaborative, everyone had input. I was one of the few people on the team with a background in 3D printing. Most of the other employees were aerospace engineers. I learned a lot from them by asking questions about how things—objects, materials, technologies—behave in space." Made In Space hired her full-time as a business development associate. She and her colleagues were challenged to figure out how to sell their 3D printing services to aerospace and

INTERNATIONAL SPACE STATION

Since 1998 the ISS *(below)* has been the largest structure that humans have launched and maintained in space. This orbiting satellite is a laboratory for new technologies. It's a great place for observation too. So astronomical, environmental, and geological research also takes place on the ISS.

About the size of a football field, the space station flies at an altitude between 205 and 255 miles (330 and 410 km) above Earth. It circles Earth almost sixteen times per day at a speed of about 17,500 miles (28,160 km) per hour. It can be seen from Earth without a telescope. Space agencies from the United States, Russia, Europe, Japan, and Canada are responsible for maintaining the ISS.

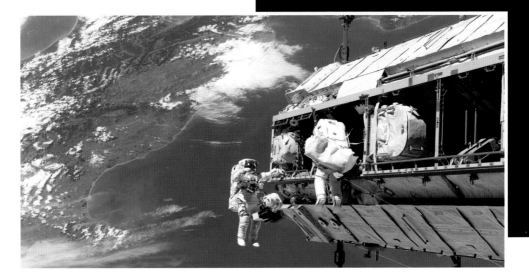

research labs around the world. These organizations want to know how their designs will print and work in space. Printing in space, at zero gravity, is tricky. Afsarifard had to figure this out. And she had to estimate how much time an astronaut in space would need to print prototypes, including tools and replacement parts.

She says that she and her team encountered many roadblocks as they developed an approach to printing tools and parts in space. For example, the National Aeronautics and Space Administration (NASA) had to first approve the safety of each prototype design. This takes time. Yet 3D printing and start-up culture are about speed. The space industry is about being careful and precise. Often products in the space industry are delayed for months or even a year or more. Afsarifard and her team kept moving forward, making sure that NASA had what it needed so that the 3D printing-in-space projects could be successful.

A team tests the Made In Space zero-gravity 3D printer in the Microgravity Science Glovebox (MSG) facility at Marshall Space Flight Center. The complex is in Huntsville, Alabama, and is the site where NASA tests new rocketry and spacecraft technologies.

One big project was to develop the Zero-G Printer. Since outer space has no gravity to hold things in place, astronauts at the ISS need a printer that can function outside of the pull of gravity. But a study found that the materials for 3D printing are toxic. The Made In Space team asked themselves, "Do we want these materials in an enclosed space station system where astronauts are breathing in these toxins? Of course not." So what did they do? They made a filtration system that filters out toxins from the air. The system actually makes the air quality on the ISS better.

The Made In Space team also created the Material Recycler (R3DO) to complete the ISS printing system. Waste materials from previous print jobs could be melted down and turned back into 3D printing materials. The whole system was launched into space on September 21, 2014. Afsarifard says, "Materials used in 3D printing are going to have a big impact on how Earth friendly 3D printing really is. At Made In Space, we were able to make a closed loop, sustainable system (nothing wasted, no toxins). On Earth, we have more comforts and access to resources so we tend to let environmental concerns slide. The 3D printing industry will need to be intentional about the 3D printing materials used anywhere, whether they are on Earth or in space, so that they are not toxic and that they can be reused or recycled."

Afsarifard says the technology and business model for Made In Space is challenging—and rewarding. Her favorite challenge was helping to develop the Future Engineers program. This educational program is for young people aged five to eighteen to design a space tool. In this yearly competition, participants learn 3D modeling and printing, specifically for making space tools and other objects that astronauts need. The winners' tools go to the ISS, where astronauts print them on Afsarifard's 3D printer. She says, "3D printing is a very intuitive technology for kids. And it is getting more so. Kids growing up with 3D printing are going to think about the world so differently."

Her advice? "I'm very inspired by people who have an idea and make it a reality. If you see something and it's not already happening, why not make it happen?"

Afsarifard no longer works for Made In Space. But she continues to be a 3D innovator, educator, and business developer.

HOW DO YOU GET ACCESS TO 3D PRINTING?

Hasti Afsarifard and many others in her field want everyone to have access to 3D printing. It is becoming more affordable over time. So one option is to buy your own 3D printer and learn how to use it. But there are other options. Soon you will be able to go to your local printshop and get your 3D-printed object as easily as you can print anything you want on paper. In many cities, you already can. Here's where to look for a 3D printer near you:

YOUR LOCAL LIBRARY. Many libraries have bought 3D printers as a way to draw people into the library. Contact your local library to see if it or any other branches have 3D printers you can use. Ask about free classes on 3D printing that the library might offer.

YOUR LOCAL UPS STORE. UPS has 3D printers in many of its stores in the United States. Check the UPS website to find the nearest UPS store.

YOUR LOCAL 3D HUBS. 3D Hubs is a website that will help you find and use a 3D printing service company near you. Check it out!

SHAPEWAYS. This website offers many possibilities. You can choose from a range of predesigned items. Or you can design your own item and use the website's design services to customize it. Or Shapeways will print your design or model. With Shapeways, you can print stainless steel, precious metals, various plastics, and more in full color or monochrome (one color). Shapeways also has a large online marketplace where you can sell and buy 3D-printed items.

MAKEXYZ. This site connects people who have print-ready designs to people who have the 3D printers to print the items. Through MakeXYZ, you can upload your design to be 3D printed. MakeXYZ will also help you find a local 3D printer. Or you can provide 3D printing services yourself through MakeXYZ.

YOU3DIT. You3Dit can help you design and 3D print whatever you want. You don't have to come with a design, just an idea. You3Dit designers will work with you to create the model and get it printed. They can also help you print a model that you created yourself.

Besides 3D printers, the site provides other fabrication tools, such as laser cutters and etchers. You3Dit connects you with a local fabricator or 3D printing service to produce your model. Or if you are a designer or have your own 3D printer, you could list your services with this site.

You can also find online libraries of 3D designs that you can print as is or customize. Here are a few resources to get started:

THINGIVERSE. MakerBot started Thingiverse, an online design community for discovering, making, and sharing 3D printable things and to encourage creating and remixing 3D designs and 3D printing. All designers are encouraged to make their designs available through a Creative Commons license. This type of license allows anyone to use a design as is or change it, without asking permission to do so or paying a fee.

3D WAREHOUSE. The 3D Warehouse name says it all. At this site, you can find a variety of 3D printable files.

SKETCHFAB. This site offers a multimedia platform to share 3D designs. You can publish and find 3D content. The site also offers virtual reality content.

Your local library may be one place to learn more about 3D printing. Check to see if the library in your neighborhood has printers and classes.

CHAPTER 6

3D PRINTING OUR FUTURE

"The interesting thing about 3D printing is that it doesn't replace one manufacturing industry, it could replace them all," says Adrian Bowyer, inventor of RepRap. Other people think that 3D printing is a limited form of manufacturing. For example, the *Harvard Business Review* wrote in a June 2015 article that "technological limitations, high material costs, lack of safety and quality standards, and high energy costs [limit] 3D printing to specialized situations . . . and complex products."

The reality for 3D printing may lie somewhere in the middle. It may complement traditional manufacturing as well as manufacture its own innovations. Amir Sasson writes in the online *Business Review* that "3D printing will not reshape the manufacturing landscape completely." Instead, he believes that 3D printing will inspire new approaches to manufacturing and new business opportunities.

Chuck Hull, one of the inventors of 3D printing, probably has the most realistic view: Time will tell. In an interview, he said, "The speed and the cost effectiveness of 3D printing are constantly moving. Over time [3D printing and 3D

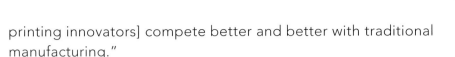

printing innovators] compete better and better with traditional manufacturing."

Meanwhile, 3D printing is evolving rapidly. In medicine many scientists around the world are designing and discovering how to bioprint customized organs to implant into the human body. In clothing, engineers, designers, and technologists are creating pieces that communicate with our bodies. In architecture, engineers, architects, and technologists use 3D printing to design and build new structures on Earth and in space. In aerospace, automotive, and energy industries, engineers and designers use 3D printing to produce new parts that make things lighter, stronger, faster, and more efficient.

Experts don't agree on whether 3D printing will take over traditional manufacturing. But they do agree that it will radically reshape the way we design and produce goods.

A common theme for all future uses of 3D printing is design. A design shows the plan for how something will look and function. In traditional manufacturing, a person or group determines the design. In 3D printing, the computer can help with the design too. In other words, a human can create and manipulate a design on a computer. The computer can manipulate the design to modify and improve it. This coordination between a human and the software design creates new possibilities for how an object will look and how it will behave.

CARLOS OLGUIN AND PROGRAMMABLE MATTER

Carlos Olguin is an entrepreneur and self-proclaimed geek with a passion for the future of 3D printing digital materials. He grew up in the 1980s in Mexico City, Mexico. From a young age, Olguin loved to program computers and to see patterns in the natural world around him. He was interested in how computers work and how the physical world, including the human body, work. He saw a relationship between the two. Both computers and the natural world have rules and follow patterns. Olguin's parents are agricultural researchers. They specialize in helping people wisely use the resources around them to grow crops that are good for Earth and for people. Their work fostered his interest in the physical world.

> ## 66 THE [PROGRAMMABLE] OBJECT YOU DESIGN GETS ITS INITIAL STATE FROM 3D PRINTING. YOU ARE PRINTING AN INCOMPLETE DESIGN THAT CONTINUES TO EVOLVE AFTER IT'S PRINTED."
>
> —Carlos Olguin, 3D printing entrepreneur

In college and graduate school, Olguin explored systems—the patterns of how things work together. He explored systems in the two areas he cares about most: computer science and biology. He earned degrees in networked computer systems from Carnegie Mellon University in Pittsburgh, Pennsylvania, and from Monterrey Institute of Technology and Higher Education (ITESM) in Monterrey, Mexico. He also took graduate courses in molecular biology systems at Columbia University in New York and at the University of Gothenburg in Sweden.

For Olguin the two worlds of biology and computer science came together with 3D printing in 2011. That year he started the

Bio/Nano Research group at Toronto-based Autodesk Research. Autodesk works with universities and tech companies to develop software for 3D designs in a range of industries from medicine to entertainment. Autodesk research groups create and improve products for these industries.

Olguin's biology/nanotechnology (bio/nano) group works with programmable matter—any material that can change its shape or other characteristics through codes programmed into it. The bio/nano group also designs a range of 3D tools. These include a molecular viewer that allows medical researchers to view viruses and other microscopic structures in the human body— on a computer screen and in 3D. At Autodesk, Olguin was an intrapreneur, an employee who takes an idea and makes it into a product the company can sell.

Olguin and his coworkers designed software called Project Cyborg. With Project Cyborg, anyone who has large amounts of data can let the data create the design. For example, the data could be millions of molecules or other biological structures.

SELF-ASSEMBLY LAB AT MIT

In self-assembly, a set of parts interact with one another to build a structure without guidance from an outside source. At the Self-Assembly Lab at MIT, designers, engineers, and scientists work together to invent self-assembly and programmable material technologies. Examples include furniture that can build itself when water is added. Or it could be a cell phone that builds itself as the parts come together on their own. These projects will change how we construct, manufacture, and assemble products and how these products perform.

The software combines these structures in numerous ways to reveal the ideal design to the designer. Olguin says, "It's more about setting rules for interaction among the individual parts, from which a design emerges."

Using the software, scientists and technologists can simulate possibilities using mathematical models with any of the materials they work with. These materials can be at the nano level (measured in super-tiny nanometers) or at the much larger human level. From these models, users can write a computer program for a designed object to be 3D printed.

With programmable matter and software such as Project Cyborg, the design of a 3D-printed object can evolve even after it is printed. Take wood grain as an example. Olguin and Autodesk coworkers collaborated with the Self-Assembly Lab at MIT to create 3D printable furniture that can be shipped flat and assembled later by the buyer. The key is to use customized wood grains. Depending on a wood's natural grain pattern, it will fold in different ways when water is added.

Olguin explains: "Material A expands in the presence of the water, material B does not. We create a specific arrangement of these two materials so that a specific shape emerges. In a way, everything around us is programmable since any material behaves according to a set of rules of interaction all the way to the nanoscale and below." In the furniture example, a customer could order a programmable piece of furniture online, print the material on a 3D printer, add water, and watch the piece of furniture take shape according to the instructions in the programmable materials.

In 2015 Olguin left Autodesk to start his own company, BioINK. BioINK produces programmable, temporary tattoos. These temporary tattoos are 3D printed onto the body to alert a person of important information. For example, the tattoo would alert epileptics that they are about to have a seizure. Or it could let diabetics know that their insulin levels are too low before the person becomes ill.

ARCHITECTURE

Skylar Tibbits is an architect, designer, and computer scientist. He codirects the Self-Assembly Lab at MIT. He and his team program instructions into the digital objects and building structures that they create. Once they are 3D printed, these objects and structures can assemble, replicate (copy), or repair themselves on-site because of their programmed instructions. For example, the lab has designed and 3D printed water pipes that can sense the need to expand or contract. If you live where winter temperatures are far below freezing, you'll see the benefit of these pipes. They won't burst and flood your house when it gets supercold outside! Instead, they will sense the dangerous cold and get the water flowing so it doesn't freeze. Tibbits says, "Imagine if our buildings, our bridges, machines, all [the elements of our structures] could actually compute." These computing features come in handy in extreme environments, such as outer space, or in hard-to-reach places, such as pipes in the walls.

NASA wants to create homes for humans on Mars by the year 2030. As part of this effort, NASA launched a competition to develop, design, and build a habitat for deep space using 3D printing technology. The team at RedWorks, a start-up in Lancaster, California, was inspired by the NASA challenge. To get started, RedWorks founder Keegan Kirkpatrick realized he needed experts from a variety of fields. So he brought together a geologist who understands the materials available on Mars, a 3D printing specialist who had formerly focused on movie special effects, and a designer for translating 3D images into real-world objects. Engineers also joined the team to build a Mars habitat for NASA. Together, they invented a 3D printing system that requires three things: a 3D printer, a power source, and regolith (a layer that covers rock) from Mars. "When you heat up the regolith [using the 3D printer], it comes out like a molten taffy," Kirkpatrick explains. "Once it cools, you can make anything you want: roads, fuel tanks, a habitat."

Kirkpatrick believes he will be able to sell this 3D printing technology to companies that make structures and other items for NASA missions to Mars and other destinations in outer space. He may also be able to sell it to Earth-bound organizations such as construction companies and archaeology programs that want to rebuild ancient structures. Or he could sell it to reclamation organizations that rebuild landscapes after drilling projects are completed.

The World's Advanced Saving Project (WASP) also plans to print houses in challenging locations. The team intends to build affordable homes and entire villages in communities around the world where typical building materials (such as bricks, stones, and wood) are unavailable or too costly. WASP's 3D printing techniques use local clays and seeds from native plants. To build a house this way, a WASP team of botanical, architectural, and 3D printing experts developed a unique approach. First, a 3D printer prints a mixture of clay and seeds, layer by layer to construct a house. The seeds absorb the clay's moisture, growing and developing their root systems into the 3D-printed structure. The root systems strengthen the layered material and therefore the house.

CLOTHING

Maybe you've thought about living on Saturn. But have you thought about what you would wear besides a space suit? Neri Oxman's work may inspire you to think differently about the world of materials, including what is possible for all kinds of clothing. Oxman's research and development mix computational design, materials science, biology, and 3D printing. In fact, she calls her research field material ecology, because it is based on a relationship between material design and biology.

Oxman founded the Mediated Matter group at the MIT Media Lab in the first decade of the twenty-first century. The group researches and designs objects from natural materials that are then programmed and 3D printed into a variety of items. For example, the group used Stratasys multi-material 3D printing technology to print a small collection of wearables. Each one is made of tiny programmed microbes, designed for wear on a particular planet. Displayed at Euromold in Frankfurt, Germany, the collection is called

Designer-innovator Neri Oxman is a professor of media arts and sciences at the MIT Media Lab. She is fascinated by the intersection of computational design, digital fabrication, materials science, and biology.

Wanderers, An Astrobiological Exploration. The group created a bodice garment, called Zuhal, from bacteria that can adapt to the storms on Saturn. The bacteria on the bodice's surface would turn the planet's toxic hydrocarbons into safe, edible matter.

Oxman explains, "Traveling to destinations beyond planet Earth involves voyages to hostile landscapes and deadly environments. Crushing gravity, ammonious [poisonous] air, prolonged darkness, and temperatures that would boil glass or freeze carbon dioxide, all but eliminate the likelihood of human visitation. . . . Each wearable is designed for a specific extreme environment where it transforms elements that are found in the atmosphere to one of the classical elements supporting life: oxygen for breathing, photons for seeing, biomass for eating, biofuels for moving, and calcium for building."

The group also 3D printed a large dome called the Silk Pavilion using sixty-five hundred live silkworms. The dome is on display at MIT. It was an experiment to see if the silkworms' natural ability to make silk could be merged with a 3D approach to building a dome. The group learned that they could control the spinning patterns of the silkworms by altering the silkworms' environment. Then Oxman developed a CAD program to control the silkworms' creation. The group placed an arrangement of silk starter threads on a scaffold (support structure) to serve as a base for the worms to do their work. The group then released thousands of silkworms onto the scaffold. The animals swarmed over the structure's surface and spun silk threads that eventually formed a dome. Oxman says, "In more than one way, a silkworm is a sophisticated multi-material . . . 3D printer."

BIOPRINTING

Scientists and engineers around the world continue the quest to bioprint human organs for use in the real world. Experiments

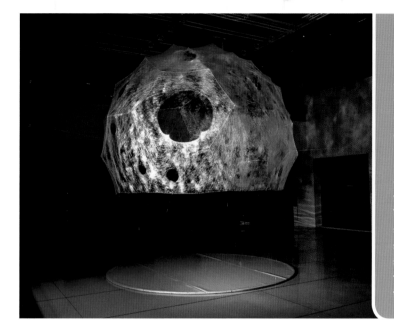

Neri Oxman and her team at MIT Media Lab's Mediated Matter Group were inspired by the way silkworms weave delicate cocoons from a single strand of silk. So they created the Silk Pavillion using a base of robot-woven threads wrapping a steel frame. Then they released sixty-five hundred live silkworms onto the structure to spin more threads to complete the dome.

to discover how to 3D print organs that can function in the human body abound.

Many universities and several organizations have developed technologies for printing human tissues. Others focus on vascular (blood) systems that would help 3D-printed tissues function. Bioprinters have successfully re-created human ears, noses, skull bones, jawbones, skin sections, bladders, arteries, and fat. While 3D-printed functioning organs, such as hearts, may be many years away, other parts of the body that also require function and growth may be just a few years away.

The following stories showcase just a sample of bioprinting research:

HEART

Imagine being able to print a beating heart. Adam Feinberg, associate professor of materials science and biomedical engineering

MATERIALS FOR THE FUTURE

Materials will play a major role in the future of 3D printing. Technologists and scientists are not limited to plastics, resins, or powders. They are exploring the boundless possibilities of 3D-printed materials such as these:

- **LOCAL MATERIALS** such as sand, soil, clay, and rock can be used to print homes and other buildings. They cost less, use less energy, and waste less than traditional manufacturing.

- **PROGRAMMABLE MATERIALS** are more efficient. They allow materials to work in new ways, following the rules designers encode into them.

- The natural behaviors of **BIOLOGICAL MATERIALS,** such as bacteria and insects, influence and can be programmed to influence the construction and durability of a finished product.

- **HUMAN CELLS** can create human organs for transplants. This can reduce the risk of the body rejecting the new organ. And it can mean that transplant patients no longer have to wait for a vital organ. The waiting time for an organ will no longer be a matter of life and death.

- **MULTIPLE MATERIALS IN ONE OBJECT.** Functionally Graded Rapid Prototyping (FGRP) allows designers to use different materials in one 3D-printed object. For example, Carpal Skin is a 3D-printed prototype created by Neri Oxman and her team for medical use. The wearable brace is made from acrylic composites (clear plastic). It has differing thickness, elasticity, and textures. The brace helps stabilize the arm. People with wrist and hand pain from repetitive work, such as typing on a computer, get relief.

at Carnegie Mellon University in Pittsburgh, Pennsylvania, has come up with a technique to print heart tissue. Once damaged due to a heart attack or other illness, heart tissue does not repair itself. Feinberg and his team have developed a technique to print a functional human heart. They modified a MakerBot printer and used open-source hardware and software to achieve their goals. To print an artery or a full heart, they start with MRI scans of human coronary (heart) arteries and 3D images of hearts.

Heart tissue is naturally soft, so a printed heart must be soft too. One of the challenges of printing with soft materials is to support the print layers so they do not move while the printer adds the next layer. The team's solution was to make a gelatin slurry (semiliquid) made from several chemicals to support the soft material. The gelatin slurry looked like warm Jello with some sand suspended in it. They printed an artery from gel made of algae. The printer squirted it into the gelatin slurry through a syringe. When the printing is complete, the printer melts the support gelatin slurry to body temperature, leaving the algae artery intact. The printer can then deposit layers of live human heart cells onto or into the algae artery scaffold. In the future, this technology could be used to repair heart tissue, to test drugs on heart tissue before approving the drugs for patient use, or to develop an entire heart for transplant.

BONES

Nina Tandon is the CEO of EpiBone, a bone reconstruction company in Brooklyn, New York. She and her coworkers have found a way to grow bones from human stem cells. Stem cells are a type of cell that can become a different type of cell within the body. Stem cells can help repair other cells.

In the recent past, bone replacement surgery looked a bit like a Frankenstein movie. Surgeons used bones from dead animals or humans to replace a live patient's bones. The patient's body would often reject these foreign bones, resulting in major complications and even death. EpiBone has a new approach the company hopes can become a reality: use a patient's stem cells and a 3D printer to grow new bones for the patient. The process involves four main steps:

Step 1: An EpiBone technician takes a CAT scan of the patient's bone that needs repair. From the scan, the technician creates a personalized 3D-printed scaffold of the exact shape of the bone.

Step 2: An EpiBone technician extracts stem cells from the patient's fat and injects them into the 3D-printed scaffold.

Step 3: The stem-cell-infused scaffold is then placed into a bioreactor chamber for three weeks. The bioreactor is a growth chamber that imitates the condition of the human body (temperature, humidity, acidity, and nutrient composition). In the chamber, the stem cells grow into osteoblast cells, or bone-growing cells.

Step 4: After three weeks, a new bone has formed. It is ready for a surgeon to implant into the patient's body. Researchers hope that replacement bones made from the patient's own cells may greatly reduce the chance of the patient's body rejecting the new bone. Implants of replacement bones in humans are planned for the future.

Tandon comments on the role that she and other scientists and engineers see for cells in the 3D printing world. "No longer . . . the passive subjects of treatments, cells are now active agents. They are collaborators. And they are the kind of naturally powerful actors that you really want on your team."

TRACHEA

Remember Kaiba Gionfriddo and the bioabsorbable stent for his trachea? A 3D-printed trachea would replace the need for a tracheostomy and the stent. It would help patients who have obstructed (blocked) upper airways or other damage to their windpipe.

Dr. Faiz Bhora is chief of thoracic (chest) surgical oncology (cancer) at Mount Sinai Roosevelt and Mount Sinai St. Luke's Hospitals in New York City. He is working to 3D print a trachea from human stem cells. A trachea is made of cartilage (connective tissue). Just like any transplanted organ, an implanted trachea would need to grow as the patient grows. For a patient's body to accept a new trachea, researchers believe the organ must be grown from that person's stem cells. For a precise fit, the organ would be 3D printed.

Bhora begins the 3D printing process by putting a gel into a bioprinter. The UV light hardens the gel to create the trachea scaffold. Bhora then injects the scaffold with human stem cells. He adds signaling compounds (chemicals) to the scaffold to instruct the cells to grow into cartilage cells. Once the trachea is fully formed, the team would implant it into the patient.

As a test, the team implanted a printed trachea into a baby pig. The pig has grown into an adult with no complications from its implant. Bhora hopes to gain FDA approval for the first 3D bioprinted trachea within the next few years. With FDA approval, surgeons could implant 3D-bioprinted tracheas in humans.

While 3D soft materials continue to develop, so do hard materials in the aerospace, automotive, and energy industries. Engineers and designers are using 3D printing to produce new parts that make machines lighter, stronger, faster, and more efficient to build.

AEROSPACE

Using 3D printing, aerospace engineers have designed airplane parts that require less material to do the same job as earlier manufactured versions of the same parts. The 3D printing prototype design makes this possible. So does the 3D additive (versus traditional subtractive) process. The 3D-printed parts make airplanes lighter and more fuel efficient than traditionally manufactured aircraft. And the parts last much longer too.

Spacecraft manufacturers are also using 3D printers to make fuel tanks for satellites. The printers deposit layers of titanium, layer after layer, on a round, wheel-like platform that looks something like a potter's wheel. Lockheed Martin, a major aerospace manufacturer, bought a $4 million 3D printer in 2015. The printer can make the round satellite fuel tanks, which are each the size of a 5-foot-tall (1.5 m) ball. The printer can do the job in much less time than traditional manufacturing. So the printer reduced the cost of making the tanks by half. With approval from NASA and the US Air Force, this technology will be used for satellites, likely by 2025.

AUTOMOTIVE

Canadian manufacturer Kor Ecologic wanted to develop a 3D car. The company came up with a plan to make the Urbee 2. It takes about twenty-five hundred hours (about 104 days!) to print the car's interior and exterior on a set of Stratasys Fortus 900mc 3D printers. Urbee 2 is shaped like a water drop—one of the most aerodynamic shapes possible. The vehicle has a hybrid, 10-horsepower engine. It stores electrical energy in onboard batteries to power electric motors. And it uses chemical energy from ethanol to power the engine. In theory, the car could travel from San Francisco to New York—about 2,900 miles (4,667 km)— on only 2.6 gallons (10 liters) of ethanol.

In January 2015, US president Barack Obama inspected a 3D-printed Shelby Cobra car during a tour of Techmer PM. The Tennessee-based company makes colors and additives for the plastics and fiber industries. Techmer and Oak Ridge National Laboratory worked on the car together. The lab, run by the US Department of Energy, researches and develops a range of new technologies.

ENERGY

Dean Kamen, founder of FIRST Robotics, runs the engineering innovation company DEKA in Manchester, New Hampshire. He and his team have developed an engine—the Stirling engine—that will bring electrical power to remote, off-the-electrical-grid areas around the world. They plan to develop a water purifier that could run off this engine. The purifier will be useful for people without clean drinking water. For their 3D-printed projects, DEKA uses complex geometries (three-dimensional structures, often with gaps or hollow spaces that are difficult to produce using traditional manufacturing). They also use a nickel-based alloy metal, which works well with 3D printers.

DEKA engineers and designers want to have the best design ahead of their competitors. "The [worry] is always that there is an even better design . . . that we're not able to see yet because we are still locked into traditional ways of thinking about parts," says machine shop manager BJ Lanigan.

CHAPTER 7

DISRUPTING AND DEMOCRATIZING MANUFACTURING

Disruptions happen all the time, right? People interrupt one another, a rainstorm washes out a game, or a tragedy strikes a community. We think of disruptions as negative. But disruptions can be positive too. They can lead to changes that help people. For example, maybe a person shows everyone a new way to do something. Or a student shares an idea that's different from what the textbook or anyone else has said. In technology, disruptions often lead to new ideas and new ways of working.

By changing how we manufacture things, 3D printing is a disruptive technology. Along with those changes, 3D printing is creating new jobs. According to Engineering.com, skilled 3D printing-related jobs soared 1,384 percent from 2010 to 2014. The 3D jobs most in demand are industrial and mechanical engineers and software developers. These jobs span many fields, such as biomedical, dentistry, software, robotics, and transportation. 3D printing jobs are available at a range of companies, from large manufacturers to small employers. And 3D printing jobs are very flexible. They allow people to work for themselves or for someone else. Terry S. Yoo, head of the 3-D Informatics Group at the US National Library of Medicine, in Bethesda, Maryland, says, "The entire field is diverging, branching, and evolving as fast as any evolutionary [changing] technology you can possibly imagine."

It's exciting to think about the new types of jobs and all the new things that people can make with 3D printing to solve important problems. Traditional manufacturing limits who can make things and for whom. But with 3D printing, anyone can make anything anywhere for anyone. Some experts call this shift the democratization of manufacturing. With this radical change, 3D printing disrupts how society manages the production of products. Challenges do come, in three main areas:

Disruptive technologies such as 3D printing radically change the way we do things. They can lead to the loss of jobs as well as to new kinds of work.

- **Intellectual property.** How do we ensure that the person or people who designed a product, built it, or both get recognition and proper payment for the work?
- **Product liability and safety.** How do we make sure that products are safe to use? How do we know who made the product? Who is responsible if something goes wrong when a consumer uses a 3D-printed product?
- **Criminal activity.** How can we make sure that 3D printing doesn't help criminals in unlawful activity?

INTELLECTUAL PROPERTY

Intellectual property (IP) laws in the United States date back to our earliest history as a new nation. IP laws prevent people from using work created or invented by someone else without the owner's permission and without paying for that permission. The authors of the US Constitution felt strongly about regulating intellectual property to protect the rights of innovators. The framers of the Constitution drafted these protections into the document, which says, "The Congress shall have Power . . . To promote the Progress of Science and useful Arts, by securing for limited Times to Authors and Inventors the exclusive Right to their respective Writings and Discoveries." Some lawyers and technologists in the twenty-first century fear that technologies such as 3D printing that enable the freedom for people to create whatever they want, "may become the new normal and IP protection may go the way of the dinosaur."

Disruptive technologies such as 3D printing can change an entire industry, sometimes many industries. Think of the Internet. It profoundly changed the way publishers make and distribute books and other print material. It also radically changed the way students do research for school reports! In the twenty-first century, anyone with access to a smart device can easily get to and read information online from writers and publishers all over the world. You can buy, borrow, and even make your own book online—and sell it through online retailers. The Internet changed other businesses too, such as news, music, movies, and the sale of retail goods. These changes have an impact on intellectual property laws.

Music and IP laws are a great example. Most people before the year 2000 listened to music on the radio or on CDs that they purchased at stores. They couldn't yet access a digital file on the Internet to listen to whatever they wanted. Music publishers and radio stations took care of IP rights. Only copyrighted music was available for sale to consumers at brick-and-mortar stores. All musicians and studios received payment for their creations.

In 2000 a company called Napster posted a wide range of music online—without worrying about copyright laws and without paying music studios or musicians. Napster allowed anyone with Internet access and a computer that could play MP3 files to download and share the music for free. Music studios and musicians were outraged. A group of them, including Metallica and Dr. Dre, sued Napster for copyright infringement. The case took a couple of years to resolve. Napster was ordered to protect copyright of the music it had posted by paying millions of dollars to the copyright owners of that music. The company went bankrupt and was eventually bought by Rhapsody.

Napster's way of sharing music through online sources inspired a revolutionary new model—and a new generation of companies. We can now easily download and share music, for a fee, through online sites such as Apple's iTunes store, Amazon, and Rhapsody's Napster. These sites legally distribute music, paying studios and musicians a portion of the fees they receive.

FROM TRADEMARKS TO PATENTS

Trademarks, trade secrets, copyright, and patents are all ways to protect intellectual property. Trademarks protect brand names, logos, and product designs. Trade secrets protect techniques, such as a formula or software source code, that have value because they are secret. The formulas for Coca-Cola and for Google's search algorithm are examples of trade secrets. Copyright protects the concrete expression—such as books, music, artwork, software, and movies—of ideas. Patents protect inventions and designs.

Because of 3D printing, people are being forced to rethink copyright and patent laws. Historically, objects that are ornamental and nonfunctional, such as artwork, have been copyrightable. Objects that are purely functional, such as a toothbrush or a chair, are not copyrightable. But 3D printing makes it possible for anyone to make art that is also functional, such as unique clothing. So 3D printing companies are disrupting the definition of what is and isn't copyrightable.

The 3D companies want legal clarity on copyright issues. For example, three 3D companies—Shapeways, Formlabs, and Matter and Form—submitted a friend-of-the-court brief (a letter of support) to the US Supreme Court, in 2016, about a case between Star Athletica and Varsity Brands. These two companies make cheerleading outfits. Varsity Brands had sued Star Athletica for making outfits that they felt were too similar to those made by the industry leader, Varsity Brands itself. The question the court is trying to answer is whether the design elements (the arrangement of stripes, colors, and other patterns) on the outfits are purely functional (not copyrightable) or purely artistic (copyrightable). The letter from the 3D companies pointed out that clothing can be both artistic and functional. The case, *Star Athletica v. Varsity Brands*, doesn't directly involve 3D printing companies. But many 3D printing companies fear an unclear legal definition of copyright. They worry that without a clear

3D printing is challenging copyright and patent laws. The courts are helping decide if and how these laws might change. For example, the US Supreme Court will decide if the law protects the designs of useful items such as cheerleading outfits.

definition, the number of copyright lawsuits will increase. Inventors may become afraid to create new ideas and designs for 3D printing. The fashion industry is watching the case closely too and for the same reasons.

Some experts believe that patents can actually drive innovation. A patent protects an inventor's creation so that it can be offered to the public without fear of being stolen. If the invention is successful, it may inspire others to create new inventions that build on that invention's success. Other experts believe the opposite. They think that patents on 3D technologies prevent innovation. For 3D printing, they may be right. For example, about 225 patents for 3D printing expired between 2010 and 2014. As the patents expired, the number of industrial 3D printing companies began to grow. They doubled from thirty-one in 2011 to sixty-two in 2015. The number of desktop 3D printers that were sold also increased. About 20,000 printers were sold in 2011 compared to 278,000 printers in 2015. However, with all this innovation, the number of 3D printing patents exceeded twelve thousand in 2016. Patents can be both: a block for further innovation and an indicator—through their sheer number—of the innovation in an industry.

OPEN-SOURCE TECHNOLOGY

Open-source technology—software and hardware designs that can be used without charge, changed, and shared by anyone—is another source of innovation for the 3D printing market. Maybe you have worked on an open-source software project where you add your code to make the software better for everyone who uses it. Remember RepRap, the self-replicating printer? And MakerBot, the company that advocated for open-source products? Both of these organizations used open-source technology to expand 3D printing. They made it easy for people to experiment with

3D printing. The number of 3D printing open-source technology projects continues to grow. For example, OctoPrint provides a web interface that allows you to control and monitor your 3D print jobs from anywhere.

Companies can use both open source and IP. For example, Google has trade secrets and patents for many of its products. But it also has active open-source communities where individual developers and Google employees contribute their code to Google technologies. Google Summer of Code and Android are examples of open-source projects developed by the Google community. Time will tell how well open source and IP can coexist in the 3D printing world.

CREATIVE COMMONS LICENSE

Another approach to sharing designs more freely is a Creative Commons license. A Creative Commons license allows creators to straddle the open-source and copyright worlds. With this license, a creator retains copyright while allowing others to copy, distribute, and use their work. The Creative Commons license gives creators credit for their work. But it also encourages other people to be innovative. It is a worldwide license and lasts as long as the related copyright lasts.

PRODUCT LIABILITY AND SAFETY

Just like IP laws, consumer protection and product liability laws have been around for a long time. Product liability laws came from the innovations of the Industrial Revolution (1760–1840), which started in Great Britain. During this period, people invented machines that could mass-produce large amounts of clothing, food, automobiles, tools, and many other products in large factories. Laws at the time did not protect the safety of workers in the factories or of the consumers who bought factory-made products. For example, meat-packers in the Midwest worked in extremely unsanitary, unsafe conditions. So the beef they packaged was often filled with bacteria, making consumers dangerously ill when they ate it. Upton Sinclair's 1906 book, *The Jungle*, revealed these unsanitary practices. Americans pressured lawmakers to pass laws to ensure safe, clean working conditions. They also passed laws to encourage manufacturers to make safe and reliable products that are free of design or manufacturing defects. If a product is unsafe or the instructions and warnings are incomplete, laws make sure the manufacturer takes responsibility for any harm from that product.

The 3D printing revolution is changing manufacturing much like the Industrial Revolution did but in the opposite direction. The Industrial Revolution moved manufacturing away from individuals to large factories. The 3D printing revolution is returning manufacturing to

THE JUNGLE

New Yorker Upton Sinclair published a groundbreaking novel in 1906 that shocked the nation. He wrote about the horrific working conditions in meat-packing factories in Chicago, Illinois. In this novel *The Jungle (below)*, he described the stench of dark, unventilated rooms, where immigrant workers used sledgehammers and knives to butcher meat. They stood on floors covered with blood, meat scraps, and foul-smelling water.

Sinclair's novel outraged the American public and became an international best seller. The US Congress quickly passed the Meat Inspection Act of 1906. Another law, the Pure Food and Drug Act, outlawed false labeling of foods and drugs. This law eventually led to the 1930 launch of the FDA, which oversees the safety of foods, drugs, cosmetics, medical devices, vaccines, dietary supplements, and other products.

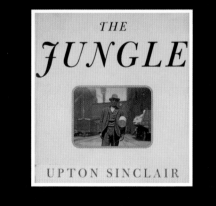

individuals. They can print what they want, wherever they want. But who is responsible for product safety? Who is responsible if a 3D-printed product fails or hurts someone?

For example, Stratasys has a design for a 3D-printed bike helmet. If someone 3D prints the helmet and it breaks, is Stratasys responsible? Is the individual who printed it responsible? What if someone modifies the Stratasys design before printing the helmet and the helmet breaks? Is Stratasys responsible? Or is the person who printed it responsible? What if the person who printed the modified design gives or sells the bike helmet to someone else? Is Stratasys responsible for the helmet's durability or is the person who printed it? Product liability laws have a long way to go to answer these questions.

Laws and regulations often fall into place only after a new technology becomes widespread. With 3D printing, for example, it is still unclear who holds legal responsibility for the safety and reliability of 3D-printed products such as this bike helmet.

CRIMINAL ACTIVITY

All kinds of things are possible with 3D printing. But should everyone really be able to make anything? What about things we know are unsafe or can cause harm to others? As examples, should anyone be able to make a drug, a weapon, or another device that harms people?

The printing of 3D guns has caused a lot of controversy. For example, Cody Wilson of Austin, Texas, posted the first design for a 3D-printed gun on a website in 2013. The US government ordered him to take down the posting. Since then a few people have posted gun designs and then been asked by Internet or 3D printing companies to remove them. Many Americans, like Wilson, feel it is their constitutional right to distribute the plans for printing guns. Others strongly disagree, believing that gun access, including the design for guns, should be regulated.

In the United States, it is legal to produce a homemade gun for your own use. US law requires a license and registration *only if* the maker of the homemade gun sells or gives the gun to someone else. A person who intends to sell or distribute a gun must have a unique serial number for the gun and register the weapon with the local police department. People who buy guns must pass a background check to complete the sale.

In the United States, it is legal for a person to own a 3D-printed gun they have made, but only for their own use. It is not legal to buy a 3D gun or to give it as a gift. US law also requires that every gun must be detectable by a metal detector. This is true for 3D guns too. If a 3D gun is plastic, it must have a metal plate that can be detected. In other countries, such as the United Kingdom and Japan, all 3D-printed guns are illegal.

US lawmakers are trying to come up with sensible laws to deal with 3D-printed guns. For example, US law regulates guns under the Undetectable Firearms Act. States and cities are coming up with laws too. California; New York; Washington, DC; and Philadelphia, Pennsylvania, have tried to ban the making or owning of 3D-printed guns in their cities. According to Janet Gilger-VanderZanden, a lawyer and writer for the Criminal Defense Lawyer website, "Because the [3D printing] technology is changing so rapidly, it is difficult to know where the law must go in order to keep the public safe, while at the same time encouraging and protecting innovation."

HEALTH AND ENVIRONMENTAL ISSUES

Safety is at stake in 3D printing for other reasons too. The US government has very strict regulations on the types of products traditional manufacturers can produce and how they make them. Many products, for example, are made with toxic materials, including plastics. And the manufacturing processes can be dangerous. Rules control how factories and workers handle and dispose of these toxic materials. Toxic plastics are used in 3D printing. But it isn't yet a regulated industry. In fact, laws and regulations for 3D printing are just beginning to develop.

TOXIC MATERIALS

Shirin Mesbah Oskui is a bioengineering graduate student at the University of California, Riverside. She discovered the health consequences of 3D-printed plastic when the zebra fish embryos she was studying in her lab began dying. She had used a 3D printer to print tools for studying the zebra fish. She didn't know why the zebra fish were dying. She and her colleagues wondered if the plastic in their 3D printer might be the cause. She decided to investigate.

The lab had two 3D printers: an FDM-based Stratasys Dimension Elite 3D printer and PLA material, and a SLA-based Formlabs Form 1+ printer and light-cured resin materials. The

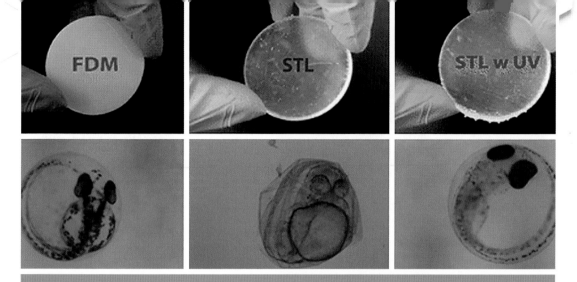

Shirin Mesbah Oskui and assistant professor of bioengineering William Grover at the University of California, Riverside, have studied the toxicity of 3D-printed parts. They used zebra fish to learn more about the chemicals used in fused deposition modeling (FDM) and in stereolithography (which the researchers labeled STL). They found that the zebra fish in their FDM and STL dishes (*left and center*) died. Those in dishes treated with UV light (*right*) survived. The study raises important questions about how to safely dispose of parts and waste materials from 3D printers.

team tested their printers. First, Oskui printed FDM and SLA 1-inch-diameter (2.5-centimeter) disc-shaped objects. Then she put zebra fish embryos and FDM-printed discs into petri dishes (small circular clear dishes with lids used to study organisms). She put SLA-printed discs into the dishes that held other zebra fish embryos. She also had a control group: zebra fish embryos in a dish without any 3D-printed plastic discs. She would compare the control group zebra fish with those in the discs with 3D-printed FDM and SLA discs.

The team monitored the three groups of zebra fish embryos to see how many eggs they hatched, how long the embryos lived, and whether any of the embryos developed abnormalities. They discovered that both the FDM- and SLA-printed discs were toxic to the zebra fish embryos. The SLA-printed discs were much more toxic. All the embryos died by the seventh day of exposure to the

WOOF MAKES A SPLASH

Many individuals and companies are going beyond making sure they create nontoxic products. They are using algae, corn, and other natural materials to make 3D-printed materials. These materials are biodegradable and often reusable. Other companies are focusing on creating filaments from recycled plastics.

The Washington Open Object Fabricators (WOOF) is part of the University of Washington's Engineering and Open 3D Printing Lab. WOOF made a splash at the 42nd Annual Milk Carton Derby in 2012. They entered a 40-pound (18 kg) 3D-printed boat *(below)* made out of recycled milk jugs. The goal was not only to reuse plastics but also to reclaim land and water from garbage overload. The group won a second-place prize.

discs. The number of zebra fish that died after exposure to FDM was slightly more than the zebra fish in the control group.

Oskui and her team had more questions. Could they do anything to make the discs safer? She developed a treatment using UV light. When the light is applied to the SLA plastic discs after they are printed, the discs become much less toxic. So Oskui put the UV-treated discs in a petri dish with zebra fish embryos. The survival rate for these embryos was almost as high as the control group. Research such as Oskui's is only the beginning of what we are learning about the hazards of 3D products and processes.

AIR QUALITY

Scientists are also investigating the connection between 3D printing and air quality. 3D printing releases toxic pollutant gases called volatile organic compounds (VOCs). It also releases tiny, dustlike nanoparticles into the air. These gases and tiny particles can settle into the lungs or the bloodstream. They can cause health risks such as breathing problems and certain cancers. Remember the Made In Space team? They realized 3D printing can pollute the air, so they created a filtration system for their outer space printer. The system ended up making the air quality on the ISS better than before the 3D printer even started printing there.

Estimates of emission rates of total nanoparticles during 3D printing are high. According to a 2013 study at the Illinois Institute of Technology, a 3D printer using PLA plastic materials releases about twenty billion particles per minute. The same type of printer using ABS materials, another type of plastic, releases about two hundred billion particles per minute. These emission rates of nanoparticles are similar to cooking on a gas or electric stove, burning scented candles, or operating laser printers.

Research on 3D printing air quality continues. So do plans to develop filtration systems for 3D printers. Until then scientists advise making sure that rooms with 3D printers are well ventilated. Ideally, use a fan that can move three times the room's volume of air in an hour. For example, if a room measures 3,532 cubic feet (100 cu. m), it should have a system that can displace 10,594 cubic feet (300 cu. m) of air in one hour. To calculate the volume of any room, measure the length, width, and height of the room. Multiply the length by the width and then by the height. That gives you the room's measurement in cubic feet. A clerk at a hardware store can help you figure out the right size of the fan for that room.

ECOFRIENDLY MANUFACTURING

3D printing has the potential to be ecofriendly. But we have to think differently to make it happen.

For example, 3D printing will lead to more damage to Earth if people bring the mind-set of "I need more" to the way they use the technology. This will lead to

- more toxic plastics because people are printing more plastic things than ever before;
- more plastic in landfills because people are treating printed plastic objects as disposable;
- more small shipments, using more fossil fuels, because people think it's OK to custom manufacture and ship individual pieces to people who order them; and
- more use of electricity because 3D printing consumes more than one hundred times as much electricity as a traditional manufacturing machine.

3D printing could help all of us tread more lightly on Earth if we think about the following:

- *Less shipping.* If we make things locally—not necessarily in our own homes but at a 3D service spot in town—we would use less fossil fuel to distribute them. Traditional manufacturing uses a lot of fossil fuels to move materials and products long distances around the globe.
- *Less waste.* If we practice "reduce, reuse, recycle" and apply it with passion to 3D printing, we can print less, reuse what we do print, fix things that we might have thrown away, and use 3D printing materials that can be recycled.
- *Less storage.* Storing 3D digital files on a computer requires less space and less impact on the environment than does storing stuff in large warehouses, which have to be heated, air-conditioned, and lit.

3D printing has the potential to cut down on waste—but only if we practice a philosophy of reduce, reuse, and recycle.

- *Less material*. Print only what you need. Typically, additive manufacturing uses less material than subtractive manufacturing. Hint: There's no extra material left over when you add because you only use as much as you need to build the object.
- *Less toxic air*. If we pay attention and create solutions, we can solve 3D air-quality and toxic-materials issues.
- *Less energy*. With 3D printing, manufacturers can create parts that have a longer life, require less energy to use, and require less frequent repairs.

A "less versus more" approach shows the potential of 3D printing to help us be kinder to our Earth. But it's not a given. We have to make it a priority and work hard to make it a reality.

TIMELINE

1983 Charles (Chuck) Hull begins to experiment with a printing method called stereolithography (SLA).

1986 Hull starts his company, 3D Systems, and receives the first patent for 3D printing using stereolithography.

Carl Deckard and Joe Beaman start DTM, a 3D printing company that sells selective laser sintering (SLS) machines.

1998 After years of experimenting with the fused deposition modeling (FDM) method, Scott and Lisa Crump start their 3D printing company, Stratasys.

2005 British engineer-mathematician Adrian Bowyer invents the RepRap printer, a machine that prints itself.

2009 Bre Pettis, Adam Mayer, and Zach "Hoeken" Smith start MakerBot with the intent to make 3D printing more accessible to the public.

2012 Max Lobovsky, Natan Linder, and David Cranor launch Formlabs with a record-breaking $3 million Kickstarter campaign.

The Washington Open Object Fabricators (WOOF) team enters a 40-pound (18 kg) 3D printed boat made out of recycled milk jugs in the 42nd Annual Milk Carton Derby. The team wins second place.

2013 Stratasys buys MakerBot and continues to make desktop 3D printers for professional, educational, and home use.

Teen inventor Alexis Lewis develops prototypes of the Emergency Mask Pod with Tinkercad (a free online CAD program) and a MakerBot Replicator.

Richard Hatfield tests the 3D printed Lightning Motorcycle at the Pikes Peak International Hill Climb. He wins by more than twenty seconds.

2014 A sustainable 3D printing system developed by Hasti Afsarifard and Made In Space launches into space for use on the International Space Station.

2015 Amos Dudley experiments with 3D printing to develop a DIY low-cost orthodontic invisible liner.

Carlos Olguin starts BioINK, which produces programmable, temporary tattoos that are printed onto the body to alert others about a person's health status.

2016 The US Supreme Court considers copyright protection for functional objects in *Star Athletica v. Varsity Brands*. The two companies make cheerleading uniforms. Several fashion associations and companies, including Formlabs, write to the court to express their desire for a clear definition of copyright.

SOURCE NOTES

6   Christine Long, "Students Use 3D Printer to Make Prosthetic Hand for Findlay Toddler," *13 ABC*, March 31, 2015, http://www.13abc.com/home /headlines/Students-use-3D-printer-to-make-prosthetic-hand-for-Findlay -toddler-298246331.html.

6   Ibid.

7   Jenny Morber, "Custom Organs, Printed to Order," NOVA *Next*, March 18, 2015, http://www.pbs.org/wgbh/nova/next/body/3d-printed-organs/.

10 Antoinette Hull to Chuck Hull, quoted in Matthew Ponsford and Nick Glass, "The Night I Invented 3D Printing," *CNN*, February 14, 2014, http://www.cnn.com/2014/02/13/tech/innovation/the-night-i-invented -3d-printing-chuck-hall.

10 Antoinette Hull, quoted in Matthew Sparkes, "We Laughed, We Cried, We Stayed Up All Night Imagining," *Telegraph* (London), June 18, 2014, http://www.telegraph.co.uk/technology/news/10908560/We-laughed -we-cried-we-stayed-up-all-night-imagining.html.

17 Travis Hessman, "Take 5: Q&A with Chuck Hull, Co-founder, 3D Systems," *Industry Week*, November 6, 2013, http://www.industryweek .com/technology/take-5-qa-chuck-hull-co-founder-3d-systems?page=3.

30 Maxim Lobovsky, interview by author, January 20, 2016.

32 Ibid.

33 Ibid.

33 Ibid.

34 Ibid.

34 Maxim Lobovsky, e-mail message to author, February 3, 2016.

35 Nadia Cheng, e-mail messages to author, February 3 and April 30, 2016.

35 Lobovsky, e-mail, February 3, 2016.

46 Amos Dudley, e-mail communication with author, June 20, 2016.

46 Ibid.

47 Maxim Lobovsky, e-mail message to author, April 28, 2016.

49 Paco Perez, quoted in Neil Koenig, "How 3D Printing Is Shaking Up High End Dining," *BBC News*, March 1, 2016, http://www.bbc.com/news /business-35631265.

50 Lynette Kucsma, quoted in Koenig, "3D Printing."

55 "3D Printing: Making the Future; Fall 2015 Donoho Colloquium—Jennifer A. Lewis," YouTube video, 1:05:12, posted by "Dartmouth," January 4, 2016, https://www.youtube.com/watch?v=ez8O_r3gLXU.

55 Jennifer Lewis, quoted in Nikita Richardson, "Most Creative People 2015: Jennifer Lewis; For Giving 3D Printing a Jolt," Fast Company, May 11, 2015, http://www.fastcompany.com/3043921/most-creative-people-2015/jennifer-lewis.

55 Richard Hatfield, quoted in "Lightning Motorcycle: Breaking the Battery Barrier," Autodesk, accessed April 5, 2016, http://www.autodesk.com/customer-stories/lightning-motorcycle.

57 Ibid.

58 Hasti Afsarifard, interview by author, March 17, 2016.

58–59 Ibid.

59 Ibid.

59 Ibid.

59 Ibid.

60 Ibid.

60–61 Ibid

63 Ibid.

63 Ibid.

63 Ibid.

66 "Selected Quotes from RepRap Inventor Dr. Adrian Bowyer," Openalia, June 5, 2012, https://openalia.wordpress.com/2012/06/05/selected-quotes-from-reprap-inventor-dr-adrian-bowyer/.

66 Matthias Holweg, "The Limits of 3D Printing," Harvard Business Review, June 23, 2015, https://hbr.org/2015/06/the-limits-of-3d-printing.

66 Amir Sasson, "Printing the 3D Future," Business Review, May 24, 2016, http://www.bi.edu/bizreview/articles/printing-the-3d-future/.

67 Chuck Hull, quoted in Hessman, "Take 5."

68 Carlos Olguin, interview by author, April 8, 2016.

70 Ibid.

71 Ibid.

71 Skylar Tibbits, "Can We Make Things That Make Themselves?," TED Talks, February 2011, https://www.ted.com/talks/skylar_tibbits_can_we_make_things_that_make_themselves/transcript?language=en.

72 Keegan Kirkpatrick, quoted in Elizabeth Segran, "RedWorks Wants to Build Your First Home on Mars," Fast Company, April 12, 2016, http://www.fastcompany.com/3058782/redworks-is-building-your-first-home-on-mars.

74 Neri Oxman, "Qamar," accessed February 20, 2016, http://www
    .materialecology.com/projects/details/al-qamar.

74 Neri Oxman, quoted in Joseph Flaherty, "A Mind-Blowing Dome Made
    by 6,500 Computer-Guided Silkworms," *Wired*, July 11, 2013, https://
    www.wired.com/2013/07/your-next-3-d-printer-might-be-filled-with
    -worms/.

78 Nina Tandon, "Lab-Grown Bones? They Could Make Painful Grafts
    History (Op-Ed)," *Live Science*, April 31, 2015, http://www.livescience
    .com/52037-lab-grown-bones-could-replace-painful-grafts.html.

81 BJ Lanigan, quoted in Peter Zelinski, "Material Improvement," *Additive
    Manufacturing*, supplement, *Modern Machine Shop*, August 1, 2015,
    http://www.additivemanufacturing.media/articles/material-improvement.

83 Terry S. Yoo, quoted in John R. Platt, "Thirty-Five Percent of Engineering
    Jobs Now Require 3D Printing Skills," *Institute*, April 3, 2015, http://
    theinstitute.ieee.org/career-and-education/career-guidance/thirtyfive
    -percent-of-engineering-jobs-now-require-3d-printing-skills.

84 U.S. Const. art. I, § 8, 1789.

84 John F. Hornick, "3D Printing and Public Policy," Finnegan, September 7,
    2015, http://www.finnegan.com/resources/articles/articlesdetail
    .aspx?news=37f63057-f52f-4466-92d3-d5016da756bf.

91 Janet Gilger-VanderZanden, "Are 3D Guns Legal?," Criminal Defense
    Lawyer, accessed May 10, 2016, http://www.criminaldefenselawyer.com
    /resources/are-3d-guns-legal.htm.

GLOSSARY

acrylonitrile butadiene styrene (ABS): a type of thermoplastic used in three-dimensional (3D) printing. It becomes soft and pliable when heated.

additive: building an object by adding one layer after another in 3D printing

algorithm: a mathematical process or set of rules that a computer can follow

bioprinter: a 3D printer that prints tissues and bones from live cell material

build platform: in non-resin 3D printing, the flat level surface, or base, onto which a three-dimensional object is built. Resin 3D printing uses a tank filled with resin instead of a build platform.

build volume: the maximum length, depth, and height of an object that a 3D printer can build; also called print volume. The bigger the 3D printer, the bigger the object it can build.

computer-aided design (CAD): software for creating digital representations of two-dimensional and three-dimensional objects

Creative Commons license: a license that allows a creator to retain a copyright while allowing others to copy, distribute, and make some use of that work. The Creative Commons license ensures creators get credit for their work while encouraging others to innovate with that work. It is a worldwide license and lasts as long as the related copyright lasts.

cure: to harden. For example, a 3D printer's ultraviolet light hardens liquid resin so that solid objects can be built.

design: the look and function of an object

entrepreneur: a person who starts a business and is responsible for the success of that business

extruder: a nozzle that deposits thermoplastic wire or other material at a precise location through a printer's printhead

fused deposition modeling (FDM): a 3D printing process of depositing heated strands of material layer upon layer to create a three-dimensional object. Fused material has been heated to a liquid or pliable state. Stratasys invented the process and owns the trademark. FDM is known as fused filament fabrication (FFF) when non-Stratasys printers use it.

fused filament fabrication (FFF): an alternative term for fused deposition modeling (FDM)

intellectual property (IP): physical creations, ideas, or processes. In the United States and globally, laws protect the owners of innovations so that other people cannot legally use those innovations or works without the owner's permission. Copyrights, trademarks, patents, and trade secrets are all legal forms of protecting intellectual property.

intrapreneur: an employee empowered by an organization to act as an entrepreneur within that organization. The employee creates something the organization can sell.

laser: light that is monochromatic (one color), coherent (one direction), and collimated (parallel) so that all of its energy is focused to produce a small point of intense power. This focused power makes laser light useful for cutting, welding, and many other things that require controlling the laser light very precisely.

magnetic resonance imaging (MRI): a scanning procedure that creates detailed images of organs and tissue within a human body. An MRI machine uses the energy of powerful magnets to create the imagery.

mathematical model: a number-based representation of how something works

mold: a container used in traditional manufacturing to give shape to hot liquids that then harden into products when the liquid cools

object file (OBJ): a file format for saving software files for 3D printing

open source: technology, usually software, the code for which is available to anyone, copyright free, to use or change in whatever way and for whatever purpose

patent: a legal document that protects owners of an invention from having their inventions used without their permission. Governments issue patents for unique creations so that people who want to make, use, or sell a patented device, process, or application must either pay the owner of the patent or get permission to do so.

photopolymer resin: a light-sensitive synthetic or organic material made of small, simple molecules chained together to form a larger molecule. Resins are similar in color to the natural sap that comes from trees and plants. Photopolymer resins in 3D printing are used to make plastics. When exposed to a printer's light, the resins harden and can be formed into objects.

polylactic acid (PLA): a biodegradable thermoplastic used in 3D printing. It is made of starch from corn, potatoes, grains, and beets.

printhead: a printer component that transfers the materials that are being used for printing onto a platform

programmable matter: any material that can change its shape or other characteristics because of the rules that a software engineer encodes or programs into it

prototype: a physical example or model of something that someone has designed. A prototype has enough of the features of the actual final product to help designers and engineers make changes to the design to perfect the final product.

rapid prototyping: a fast-paced process for creating prototypes. Because 3D printing can create prototypes quickly, the time and cost of developing a new product is reduced and therefore more affordable.

selective laser sintering (SLS): a layer-by-layer 3D printing process in which a printer's laser beam heats a solid powder in a vat, without melting the material, until the product is complete. The powder in the vat provides the support for the 3D object as it is printed, so the system does not require a platform or other type of support structure.

slicing: the process of converting (slicing) a 3D model computer file into layers. The 3D printer then interprets the layers to build a three-dimensional object.

stereolithography (SLA): a layer-by-layer 3D printing process in which the heat of a printer's laser beam cures, or hardens, a resin so it can be shaped into a solid object

stereolithography file format (STL): a software file format for 3D printing that makes a computer-aided design file readable by a 3D printer

subtractive: a process from traditional manufacturing in which an object is created from one or more pieces of material by removing the excess material

thermoplastic: a type of plastic that becomes pliable when heated and solid when cooled. ABS and PLA are examples of thermoplastics used in 3D printing.

3D: having three dimensions of width, depth, and height

ultraviolet (UV) light: a form of radiation that is not visible to the human eye. This radiation light is used in 3D printing to harden materials such as resin.

SELECTED BIBLIOGRAPHY

Barnatt, Christopher. *3D Printing: 2nd ed.* North Charleston, SC: CreateSpace Independent Publishing Platform, 2014.

Coward, C. *Idiot's Guide: 3D Printing.* New York: Penguin Group, 2015.

"Creepy but Curious: Paper Wasps." SoundCloud. Accessed March 20, 2016. https://soundcloud.com/abcnsw/creepy-but-curious-paper-wasps.

Hadley, Debbie. "How Wasps Build Wasps Nests: How Wasps Use Wood to Construct Paper Homes." About Education. Last modified October 12, 2016. http://insects.about.com/od/antsbeeswasps/qt/how-wasp-nests-are -made.htm.

Hornick, J. *3D Printing Will Rock the World.* North Charleston, SC: CreateSpace Independent Publishing Platform, 2015.

Hornick, John, and Dan Roland. "Many 3D Printing Patents Are Expiring Soon: Here's a Round Up and Overview of Them." 3D Printing Industry, December 29, 2013. http://3dprintingindustry.com/2013/12/29/many-3d-printing -patents-expiring-soon-heres-round-overview/.

Hunt, J. H. *The Evolution of Social Wasps.* New York: Oxford University Press, 2007.

Lipson, H., and M. Kruman. *Fabricated: The New World of 3D Printing.* Indianapolis: John Wiley & Sons, 2013.

Long, Christine. "Students Use 3D Printer to Make Prosthetic Hand for Findlay Toddler." *13 ABC*, March 31, 2015. http://www.13abc.com/home /headlines/Students-use-3D-printer-to-make-prosthetic-hand-for-Findlay -toddler-298246331.html.

Morber, Jenny. "Custom Organs, Printed to Order." *NOVA Next*, March 18, 2015. http://www.pbs.org/wgbh/nova/next/body/3d-printed-organs/.

"NIH 3D Print Exchange." US Department of Health and Human Services. Accessed May 20, 2016. http://3dprint.nih.gov/.

Ponsford, Matthew, and Nick Glass. "The Night I Invented 3D Printing." *CNN*, February 14, 2014. http://www.cnn.com/2014/02/13/tech/innovation/the -night-i-invented-3d-printing-chuck-hall.

"Selective Laser Sintering, Birth of an Industry." University of Texas at Austin, Mechanical Engineering, December 6, 2012. http://www.me.utexas.edu /news/2012/0712_sls_history.php.

3Ders.org. Accessed April 10, 2016. http://www.3ders.org.

"3D Printing Industry Trends." 3D Hubs. Accessed July 17, 2016. https:// www.3dhubs.com/trends.

Yong, Ed. "Paper Wasps: Caring Mothers Evolved into Selfless Workers." *National Geographic*, September 20, 2009. http://phenomena .nationalgeographic.com/2009/09/20/paper-wasps-caring-mothers-evolved -into-selfless-workers/.

FURTHER INFORMATION

Books

Diana, Carla. *LEO the Maker Prince: Journeys in 3D Printing*. Sebastopol, CA: Maker Media, 2013. LEO, a walking, talking printing robot, teaches readers about 3D printing. LEO and a character named Carla take a journey through Brooklyn, New York. Carla draws things she sees, and LEO prints them.

Drumm, Brook. *3D Printing Projects: Toys, Bots, Tools, and Vehicles to Print Yourself*. San Francisco: Maker Media, 2015. This book contains 3D printing projects that range from the simple to the fantastical. Each project requires a 3D printer, some assembly by hand, software, simple tools, basic electronics, and various inexpensive parts.

Horvath, Joan, and Rich Cameron. *3D Printed Science Projects: Ideas for Your Classroom, Science Fair or Home*. New York: Springer Science, 2016. This book describes how to create 3D printable models that can help students from kindergarten through graduate school learn math, physics, botany, chemistry, engineering, and more. Each chapter explains a science or math concept and provides a model to 3D print, using the free open-source software openSCAD. Chapter instructions explain how to manipulate a model in openSCAD so you can customize what you print. The book is for teachers, but young people can use it too to get a leg up on science fair projects—and to have fun.

Kaziunas France, Anna. *Make: 3D Printing; The Essential Guide to 3D Printers*. Sebastopol, CA: Maker Media, 2013. This book uses articles and projects from Make's print and online publications to provide everything you need to know to purchase and use a 3D printer. You'll find help on finding hardware and software as well as tips on 3D printing techniques.

Murphy, Maggie. *High-Tech DIY Projects with 3D Printing*. New York: PowerKids, 2014. This guide presents the basics of 3D printing, beginners' projects, and more to help you make what you want to make.

Otfinoski, Steven. *3D Printing: Science, Technology, and Engineering.* New York: C. Press, 2016. Discover how innovators find ways to make 3D printers smaller, easier to use, and more affordable than ever. You will also learn how 3D printing changes the way we manufacture aircraft, treat injuries, and more.

Videos

"Bambi Meets Godzilla." YouTube video, 1:30. Posted by "Galaxy fm," June 29, 2006. https://www.youtube.com/watch?v=rwnd3PY46-g. Marv Newland created this classic short, animated video cartoon in 1969. Carl Deckard and Joe Beaman created early 3D printers in the 1980s that they named Godzilla and Bambi, after the characters in this cartoon. In the film, the powerful Godzilla crushes Bambi. It can be viewed as a way to think about superpowers squashing independent individuals.

Print the Legend. Santa Monica, CA: Audax Films, 2014. http://printthefilm .com/. This documentary follows the developers of MakerBot and Formlabs as they challenge themselves and the world to bring 3D printing to the desktop. If you like the story of how Apple and Microsoft brought computing to our desktops and into our mobile lives, you'll like this film.

Websites

Many online sites offer information and tutorials about 3D printing. Others offer services and materials for purchase. These two resources provide news, designs, and ways to network in the 3D world.

Thingiverse

https://www.thingiverse.com/

This online design community helps visitors make and share 3D printable things and create and remix 3D designs and 3D printing. All designers are encouraged to make their designs available through a Creative Commons license.

3D Printing Industry

http://3dprintingindustry.com

This website is a great resource for learning about breaking trends in the world of 3D printing. Videos cover a range of topics, including entrepreneurs of all ages at work on 3D-printing projects. You can sign up for a newsletter, learn about 3D printing hardware and software, and stay up on events, awards, and new apps.

INDEX

PHOTO ACKNOWLEDGMENTS

The images in this book are used with the permission of: design:© iStockphoto. com/from2015 (hexagons shapes); backgrounds: © iStockphoto.com/ ErmanCivici (wires); © iStockphoto.com/cherezoff (printer); © John van den Heuvel/Minden Pictures, p. 5; Courtesy of Abbey Nickel, p. 6; © BSIP/UIG/Getty Images, p. 7; Hero Images Inc/Alamy Stock Photo, p. 9; © Pascal Goetgheluck/ Science Source, p. 10; Joel Koyama/ZUMA Press/Newscom, p. 12; Hero Images Inc./Alamy Stock Photo, p. 19; BSIP SA/Alamy Stock Photo, p. 21; wu kailiang/Alamy Stock Photo, p. 22; David Stock/Alamy Stock Photo, p. 24; © CHRISTOPHER GREGORY/The New York/Redux, p. 27 (top); Pakete/Alamy Stock Photo, p. 27 (bottom); © MakerBot Industries/Wikimedia Commons (CC BY 2.0), p. 29; © Dustin Finkelstein/Getty Images, p. 32; © ISAAC KASAMANI/ AFP/Getty Images, p. 37; © Chris So/Toronto Star/Getty Images, p. 39; Courtesy of Michelle Lewis, p. 41; © BSIP/UIG/Getty Images, p. 43; © Horacio Villalobos/ Corbis/Getty Images, p. 45; © ROBYN BECK/AFP/Getty Images, p. 49; Piero Cruciatti/Alamy Stock Photo, p. 51; © Richard Levine/Corbis/Getty Images, p. 54; © Voxel8, Inc., p. 56; NASA, pp. 61, 62; © Steve Debenport/Getty Images, p. 65; © Laurie Rubin/ Photographer's Choice/Getty Images, p. 67; dpa picture alliance/Alamy Stock Photo, p. 69; © Essdras M Suarez/The Boston Globe/Getty Images, p. 73; © Rick Friedman/rickfriedman.com/Corbis/Getty Images, p. 75; REUTERS/Kevin Lamarque/Newscom, p. 81; © Maciej Frolow/ The Image Bank/Getty Images, p. 83; © iStockphoto.com/RobMattingley, p. 86; © Todd Strand/Independent Picture Service, p. 89; © Stratasys, p. 90; Reprinted with permission/American Chemical Society via Copyright Clearance Center, p. 93; © Brandon Bowman/Wikimedia Commons, p. 94; Dmitry Kalinovsky/ Shutterstock.com, p. 97.

Front cover: © iStockphoto.com/Chesky_W.

Back cover: © iStockphoto.com/cherezoff.

ABOUT THE AUTHOR

Melissa Koch is a writer and inventor of digital learning environments for children, educators, and adults. She specializes in materials that encourage women and youth from diverse backgrounds to pursue their dreams in science, technology, engineering, and mathematics (STEM). Her STEM curricula activities have received recognition from the National Science Foundation, Whitehouse Science Fair, PBS, and others. She lives in the San Francisco Bay Area, with her husband, son, and Labrador retriever. She dreams of creating a 3D printer that can print both wood and metal to fix her favorite antique furniture and bicycle.